QUIET YOUR MIND

ALSO BY JOHN SELBY

Seven Masters, One Path

Kundalini Awakening

Conscious Healing

Finding Each Other

Shattering Jade

Sex and Spirit

Secrets of a Good Night's Sleep

Fathers: Opening Up

Immune System Activation

Enjoying Solitude

Peak Sexual Experience

The Visual Handbook

Couples Massage

Powerpoint

quiet your mind

JOHN SELBY

 New World Library
Novato, California

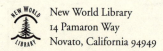 New World Library
14 Pamaron Way
Novato, California 94949

Book design by Maxine Ressler

Publisher Cataloging-in-Publication Data
Selby, John.
    Quiet your mind / John Selby.
        p. ; cm.
        Originally published in German.
        Includes bibliographical references.
        ISBN: 978-1-930722-31-6
        1. Attitude (Psychology) 2. Emotions. 3. Quality of life. 4. Mental
    health. I. Title.
BF327 .S45 2004
152.4 – dc22   0407

ISBN: 978-1-930722-31-6
Printed in Canada

20 19 18 17 16 15 14 13

Contents

the ultimate choice

For hundreds of years now, Western civilization has become more and more engulfed in the thinking mind's grand assumption that its own mental chatter and nonstop flow of judgments and worries is the most important happening on planet Earth. Ever since Descartes made his intellectual's assertion *Cogito, ergo sum* – "I think, therefore I am" – the talkative function generating our stream-of-consciousness commentary on everything happening around us has gained free reign to dominate almost every moment of our lives.

I would like to quietly yet forcefully challenge this ego assumption that we function best, and enjoy life to the fullest, when we're habitually engaged in nonstop mental reflections, worries, plottings, and judgments. In exact contrast, this book will demonstrate that only through regularly quieting the entire flow of thoughts, images, memories, and reflections that fill our minds can we regain intimate and fulfilling contact with sensory, intuitive, and heart-felt experiences that emerge when we shift into direct encounter with the world around us.

Brain scans show that the energetic functioning of our brains changes dramatically and immediately when we shift from left-brain deductive thinking to more right-brain and even whole-brain intuitive and experiential modes of consciousness. Related studies also indicate that we must choose between being absorbed in deductive verbal reasoning (a past-future function of the mind) and direct experience of the world (a present-moment function of the mind) – because it's very difficult to do both at the same time. Consciously or unconsciously, we're constantly choosing to be engaged either in thoughts about life – or in the direct experience of life.

As a first goal, the following discussions will shine a bright spotlight on this ultimate mental choice and demonstrate that maintaining a healthy balance between direct experience in the present moment, and cognitive reflection upon that experience is the ideal mental flow for a fulfilled life. We will then learn the most effective psychological techniques for shifting from thinking to experiencing on a regular basis.

Freedom from Mood Swings

Allowing our minds to be consumed in chronic thought-flows not only shuts us off from direct present-moment encounter with the world around us, but it also leaves us vulnerable to an overdose of negative emotions that can confuse our minds, stress out our bodies, and destroy any feelings of peace, joy, and transcendence. Cognitive psychology has proven that most of our upsetting emotions are directly caused not by what's going on around us, but by fear-based thoughts we're habitually running through our minds. One goal of this book is to make sure that we understand the true source of our negative mood swings—and we will learn practical and effective psychological techniques for putting aside those thoughts that pollute otherwise enjoyable and fulfilling lives.

Most of us would give a great deal to break free of the mental agitations and tensions that consume so much of our inner lives. Rather than remaining chronically fixated on often-disturbing thoughts about our worries and confusions, conflicts and frustrations, we'd certainly prefer to be enjoying the simple yet elusive qualities of mental clarity, heartfelt intimacy, inner peace, and emotional calm – not to mention the even more valuable realms of intuitive realization and bliss.

But it's often assumed that having worried chatterbox minds is just our God-given nature – that we have no choice but to accept our fate of being dominated by thought-flows that keep our emotions stirred up and our minds agitated. Many people, especially intellectuals who live almost all the time in their thinking minds, actually believe that it's impossible to quiet the flow of thoughts through their heads.

As we will explore in depth in this book, such a fatalistic assumption about our mental functioning is now known to be false. We *do* possess the inherent power to control the content of our thoughts and quiet chronic thought-flows altogether whenever we choose.

Of course, a certain amount of mental problem solving and cognitive reflection is essential to human life, and can actually be quite fun, even deeply fulfilling. Deductive thinking is an invaluable mental tool enabling us to create and maintain our entire technological civilization. Furthermore, regularly entertaining uplifting thoughts that brighten our lives, give philosophical meaning to our existence, and encourage positive feelings can be a great help in raising our spirits and spreading joy around us.

However, all too often our habitual thought-flow carries a

negative rather than a positive emotional edge, generated by old fear-based attitudes, assumptions, and beliefs that no longer correctly reflect our present reality. Predictably, such thoughts from outdated or distorted beliefs provoke anxious, aggressive, and depressive emotions – which in turn make us suffer.

Usually we're not aware of the underlying source of such mood swings. Minor or sometimes even major attacks of anxiety and anger, depression and hopelessness, inadequacy and guilt, seem to sneak up out of the blue and overwhelm us. If only we could avoid getting caught up in such mood swings, it would be a joy to wake up to life each morning.

Experiential Realms

In our pragmatic day-to-day lives, how can we act to break free from the feeling that we are helpless victims of our own negative moods and thought-flows? What is the underlying psychological process that enables us to shift from thoughts that tend to upset our lives, to a more experiential present-moment state of mind?

The professional resolution to this question has been evolving for a hundred years now, beginning with the pioneering explorations of Sigmund Freud, Carl Jung, Erich Fromm, Krishnamurti, and Wilhelm Reich, and advancing in the mid-1900s to the more present-moment approaches of Gestalt therapy, transactional analysis, reality therapy, and bioenergetics. Then in the early 1960s psychologist Aaron Beck formally documented what observant folk, especially in meditative communities throughout the world, have known for centuries: Our emotions don't emerge suddenly out of nowhere. Just the opposite, they are almost always being stimulated by habitual thoughts and related images we keep running through our minds, often at a mostly subliminal level of awareness.

From Beck's early work in cognitive psychology at the University of Pennsylvania has emerged the most successful school of therapy to date, cognitive therapy. In this inner process, patients suffering from chronic negative emotions such as anxiety and depression, anger and confusion, are taught to identify the recurrent thought-flows that stimulate these negative emotions, and to replace these negative thoughts and beliefs with more positive and realistic ones. These new thoughts in turn stimulate positive emotions, encouraging an expanding sense of inner confidence and well-being.

This general approach to therapy works very well. A study funded by the National Institute of Mental Health, just released by researchers at the University of Pennsylvania and Vanderbilt University, shows that weekly sessions of cognitive therapy over a four-month period deliver considerably higher short- and long-term success in treating depression, for instance, than traditional psychiatric treatment involving psychoanalysis and antidepressant drug medication. Furthermore, parallel studies document that self-applied cognitive therapy programs can be of lasting benefit in the treatment of nonacute anxiety and depressive conditions. Such pragmatic mental tools can be highly valuable in our lives. Throughout this book we will be employing these tools where useful.

However, as we will discover step by step, the act of replacing negative thoughts and assumptions with more positive ones doesn't in itself fulfill our deeper need for genuine peace of mind, intuitive clarity, emotional healing, and the discovery of our human potential beyond surface concepts and mental self-image. Our discussion will of necessity take up where all but the more advanced cognitive therapists leave off by demonstrating, as Einstein wisely pointed out, that we can't solve a problem using the same mental constructs that created the problem in the first place.

The more powerful and complete approach to freeing our minds from thoughts that push upsetting emotional buttons, as indeed many of the more innovative therapists are currently exploring and employing in their work, is to first evaluate and modify our underlying beliefs – and then learn to quiet our thinking minds altogether.

Primary Mind Research

The specific techniques for shifting from deductive thinking to more intuitive and experiential modes of consciousness being introduced in this book have not, of course, emerged from a vacuum. A great deal of psychological and neurological research, experimentation, and client application have given birth to the programs being taught herein. We'll consider the most important scientific studies to date, so that we gain a clear understanding of the insights that have led to the development of this new approach to mind management and personal growth.

Especially important to this book's programs were several experiments I participated in a number of years ago that, after considerable further refinement, have evolved directly into these new programs for taking charge of our minds and tapping the power and blessing of inner quiet. These NIMH-funded studies employed electroencephalographic (EEG) and physiological equipment to document how purposeful cognitive shifts in a person's thought activity (shifting from worrying, for instance, into a quiet state of mind) predictably generate parallel changes in that person's neurological activity and physiological response. These results (replicated numerous times elsewhere) demonstrated without question the direct causative link between the chronic worried thoughts we allow to run through our minds and the resulting anxious feelings we experience as negative emotions, physical stress, and general discomfort.

Seeking to further understand the mind's influence over the body and emotions, my colleagues and I at the experimental psychology division of the New Jersey Neuro-Psychiatric Institute (NJ-NPI) studied several highly advanced Indian yogis, scientifically documenting their remarkable ability to alter their bodily functions – heart rate, body temperature, blood pressure, EEG activity, blood-clotting time, sensitivity to pain, etc. – through inner mental actions.

Perhaps most importantly for the pragmatic dimensions of these present programs, I worked with scientists at the Bureau of Research in Neurology and Psychiatry to duplicate and expand intriguing Russian EEG studies in perceptual psychology, demonstrating that when a subject's visual focus (way of looking) shifts from point fixation (focusing on one object at a time) to space fixation (being aware of two or more objects at the same time), the flow of thoughts through the mind temporarily ceases altogether – as evidenced both subjectively and by EEG data.

This insight led us to develop specific perceptual-shifting exercises that anyone can do any time or anywhere, to effectively quiet the flow of thoughts through the mind and generate a present-moment state of awareness. Related studies I participated in at NJ-NPI offered yet another vital clue to the puzzle: When we focus our attention on just one bodily sensation, thoughts usually continue flowing through our mind. However, when we learn the simple mental process of fully focusing on two or more distinct bodily sensations at the same time (breathing and heartbeat, for instance, or sight and sound), all thoughts cease flowing through the mind.

This finding scientifically documented what was predicted from more subjective studies concerning the psychological procedures common to all meditative traditions – namely, that purposeful refocusing of one's mental attention in particular ways can directly and predictably quiet the flow of thoughts through the mind.

A New Heart

The first three chapters of this book, although of serious importance in explaining how our thoughts influence our lives, and how we can transcend judgmental and anxious mental habits, are actually just necessary steps to make before being ready to reap the true payoff of this book – a new lease on our own hearts.

Recent research reviewed in depth in Chapter 4 shows that the heart consists of at least 65 percent neural matter identical to the neural makeup of the brain itself. Indeed, we can speak of our heart as being our "fifth brain." Throughout the history of humankind, the oral and written literature has spoken of the wisdom of listening to our own hearts for guidance. We can now begin to understand more clearly how we do indeed feel, and even think, with our hearts. Furthermore, research has shown that our hearts broadcast a powerful electromagnetic force field that influences and interacts with the energetic projections of other peoples' hearts. This heart-based energetic interaction has been known for many thousands of years. We're just now beginning to study it with scientific tools to understand more clearly how it functions – and how we can learn to interact heart-to-heart more consciously.

A primary goal of this book is to teach specific techniques for shifting from head fixation to heart fixation in our core sense of identity and interaction with those around us. Chapter 7, with its focus on sexual relating, further develops this theme and potential.

Many of us, because of earlier emotional trauma related to romantic disasters, the loss of a loved one, and other extremely painful heart experiences, have built inner barriers that keep us habitually shut off from any heart feelings. We've developed what people call "cold hearts" in order to protect ourselves from further heart pain. From start to finish this book is aimed at helping all of us to open our hearts again, heal the old heart wounds, and learn to quiet our thinking mind so we can listen to the deeper wisdom and guidance of our genuinely intelligent hearts.

Scientifically we're just at the beginning of a major revolution in how we understand the neural interaction between the brain and the heart. We already know that it's definitely a two-way communication, with the heart sending neural messages to the brain that stimulate chemical and hormonal activity and decision making. We also know that, from a therapeutic point of view, emotional healing requires an integration of feelings from the heart with ideas and thoughts from the cognitive center of the brain. This book takes us to the frontier of this rapidly expanding area of study.

The Benefits

When seen from a psychological and physiological point of view, the benefits of regularly letting go of past-future thinking and shifting into more present-moment modes of mind are very impressive. When we realize that, each and every moment of our lives, we have the choice between being lost in thought or fully engaged in life, the choice is quite easy to make on a regular basis.

Before we go further, let's pause and get clear together on exactly what you'll gain in your life, by mastering the set of "quiet mind" techniques being taught in this book:

COGNITIVE CALM In the very act of quieting the flow of thoughts through your mind, you'll find that you encourage a special state of inner peace and mental calm. When the constant chatter of your inner commentator ceases its chronic judging and evaluating of everything happening around you, you're free to be fully here in the present moment, relaxed and enjoying whatever's happening.

PHYSICAL PLEASURE While you're lost in thought, you're simply not present in your body – because thought takes you immediately off into the past and the future, away from your physical presence altogether. When you shift from thinking to experiencing, you tap directly into the ultimate source of all human pleasure – your own body.

HEART AWAKENING You only experience the primal positive feeling of love flowing through your heart when you're focused on the experiential present moment. When you're head-tripping you are clearly out of touch with your heart. As you consciously choose to return your focus again and again to the sensory here and now, you more actively engage your heart in the world around you, and welcome more love into your life.

INTUITIVE BRILLIANCE The predominantly left-hemisphere deductive mind moves chronically from point to point, detail to detail, securely locked away from any sudden flashes of insight and inspiration. Only when you momentarily shift out of cognitive-thinking mode do you gain access to more right-hemisphere realms of integration and intuitive brilliance where you see the whole at once and realize the deeper solution to your situation.

ANXIETY REDUCTION Almost all of your worrying is a direct result of the negative anxious thoughts habitually running through your deductive mind. As soon as you learn to actively quiet your worrying mind and emerge into the here and now, you effectively break the grip of anxiety on your soul. You let go of all the disturbing memories of things that happened to you in the past. You stop imagining all the horrible things that just possibly might happen to you sometime in the future – and thus enter the bliss and joy of engaging in the continual unfolding of the present moment.

BUSINESS SUCCESS Even in formal business circles the personal power, mental clarity, and business insight that comes from participating in the dynamic flow of the present moment is being acknowledged and encouraged. Business folk are rediscovering what sages of old have always known – that genuine success comes to you most predictably when you're tuned into what's happening right now around you, where you can respond spontaneously with your whole being rather than being held back by plans made somewhere in the past. Furthermore, relating with an open heart establishes business relationships that form the foundation of long-term success.

LIFE POSSIBILITIES Each new moment is alive with a great many choices and opportunities if you're living consciously in the present moment. But as long as you're overly goal-oriented, plotting and planning your future well in advance, you miss out on every bright opportunity that doesn't fit into your past-future projections of who you are and what you're doing in life. As soon as you commit to living in the present moment as much as possible, your life expands with untold new choices that lead in richly rewarding directions.

SEXUAL POTENTIAL Most of us tend to make love with our thinking minds still very much actively engaged: We're busy talking to ourselves about what's happening; we're anticipating what our sexual partner wants; we're telling ourselves what to do and not to do; we're worrying about whether we're satisfying our partner; we're sometimes even thinking about what we need to get done after we make love. Only when you let go of all thinking and tune into your body, heart, and soul in the present moment, does real sexual intimacy awaken within you.

HEALTH AND VITALITY Your physical health is directly undermined by chronic negative thinking, which in turn provokes tensions and stress that can seriously disturb your immune system. By learning to live more deeply in the here and now, you can reduce physical stress and thus return your body to its natural healthy state. There's nothing more revitalizing than spending relaxed time in the here and now, where the flow of healing love and pleasure can begin to wash away all the contamination of negative thoughts. You need to consciously be present in your body in order to get and stay healthy.

THE DIVINE All meditative practices teach that direct engagement with the here and now offers us our primary encounter with the divine in human life. Therefore nurturing a quiet mind, and opening our hearts to present-moment experience, is a primary prerequisite of the spiritual path. In mystic terminology, spirit isn't a phenomenon of our personal memory banks or our imaginations of a projected future. Spirit *flows in* through our hearts only when we are "here" in the present moment. We tune into spiritual guidance not while we're busy "talking to" God, but rather, when we're quiet and receptive in our minds. It's crucial to realize, as we'll explore in this book, that if we want to know God directly, we need to stop thinking about spiritual ideas, shift into "receive" mode, and encounter the genuine mystic experience – right here and now.

A New Learning Experience

Given the direct benefits of learning to quiet our minds, the motivation to continue reading this book is obvious. Reading about a new way to advance our lives is definitely an essential step toward accomplishing that expansion. We need to develop a conceptual understanding of such a process before moving into actually experiencing and mastering the process itself. Learning something new almost always involves a cognitive conceptual phase.

But how can we move beyond the "talk about" discussions and actually have the experience being described? Almost all of us have suffered the frustrating experience of reading an inspiring self-help or spiritual book, then feeling stuck with the unfulfilled desire to go the next step with the author – to close our eyes and listen directly to the author's voice guiding us personally through the actual experience we've just read about.

I have personally felt impatient writing self-help and spiritual books that lead readers conceptually toward embracing a new experience – but then leave them without the direct audio guidance I provide for my own clients and students that leads them effortlessly into the actual experience itself. This frustration has led me step-by-step to the creation of a qualitatively new self-help delivery system, combining the still-essential written text, which delivers the fundamental concepts needed to understand a new experience, with instant access (assuming you have a computer) to the audio guidance I regularly provide my clients.

So each time in this book that you come to a section presenting the actual guidance needed for experiencing a new procedure, you will find, along with the printed words, an Internet address (www.johnselby.com) that immediately takes you to a streamed-audio or downloadable program of my voice guiding you through the process. You can go online whenever you want personal guidance, close your eyes, and relax into an intimate experience of the process being learned. For those of you who do not have access to a computer, or who want to listen to the audio guidance away from your computer, there is a CD version of the audio programs described at the end of this book. You will also find me online ready to answer whatever questions regarding particular issues you want elucidated.

Jumping In

Even before we move into Chapter 1, let's focus on experiencing directly the primary process of this book – that of helping you redirect your mind's power of attention, to shift your mental functioning away from concepts, memories, imaginings, and worries, toward the immediate and always new present-moment experience coming into being all around you and within you, right here, right now. This mental shifting is a learned ability, and the more you exercise your mental-shifting muscle, the better you'll get.

PAUSE AND EXPERIENCE

•

Even while reading these words, you can begin to expand your awareness in experiential directions by also becoming aware of the air flowing in and out your nose or mouth as you breathe . . . don't do anything to change your breathing. Just experience your mind's attention beginning to expand to include not only ideas and symbols but also your own body here in the present moment . . . and as you continue reading these words, and feeling the sensation of the air rushing in and out your nose or mouth, also begin to be aware of the sounds around you . . . and when you come to the end of this paragraph, see what unique experience comes to you as you close the book momentarily, and tune fully into your breathing experience . . . your whole body here in the present moment . . . the sounds . . . the colors . . .

part one

primary programs

chapter 1

who's running your mind?

Each of us is born into this world in intimate possession of a personal biocomputer so vast and mysterious that even our best scientists admit that – considering the staggering interactive complexity of the organ – they know very little about how it actually runs and what its ultimate potential might include. And the average person remains in virtual darkness concerning the neurobiology of consciousness and the underlying mental forces that shape our lives.

There's certainly no owner's manual for our brain – and our parents, who are initially in charge of fine-tuning its performance and data entry during our formative years, receive no formal training at all before taking over the massive job of orchestrating our mental and emotional development. Furthermore, we then go through at least twelve years of academic schooling, during which our minds are required to perform mental gymnastics and download great quantities of information to clog our cognitive storage units, and yet we never receive significant guidance in how to manage all the complex emotional, intuitive, perceptual, and spiritual dimensions of our mental functioning.

We know the end result: We do our very best to manage and hopefully even excel in our mental performance. And sure, we somehow survive one after another emotional and spiritual crisis. But ultimately, when we ask ourselves who's really in charge here, the answer is all too often uncertain, discouraging, or even downright scary.

When queried gently, most of us admit that we all too often feel like helpless victims of our various mood swings – for no seeming reason at all, we sometimes find ourselves engulfed in worries or even caught up in a full-blown panic attack. At other times we may sink unexpectedly into bouts of depression, or flair up with uncalled-for hostility – or perhaps find ourselves shrinking back from the world with thoughts and feelings mired in guilt, shame, apprehension, or self-loathing.

Of course most of us have our better days, when we wake up bright and eager, full of love and fun, spreading joy and laughter wherever we go. But even our brighter, more joyful moments tend to come to us not because of anything we have done consciously through wise mind management, but seemingly out of the blue. We might feel thankful for our good feelings, but still we know we're not in charge – and at any moment we can get dragged down again into another bout of negative thoughts, emotions, and physical symptoms that turn an otherwise beautiful day into a bother, or even sometimes into a living hell.

Obviously I paint this initial somewhat depressive picture of our present social condition not to further depress you, but just the opposite – to say loud and clear that such emotional suffering and mental anguish are not necessary. With the proper mental tools they can be dealt with directly and consciously put aside.

As a psychologist who has been studying mood swings and their underlying cognitive causation for thirty years now, I can say emphatically that chronic emotional suffering is not our natural state, nor is it our necessary destiny. Yes, something is haywire inside our collective minds; somewhere during the development of our giant thinking brains still wedded to ancient survival emotions, we missed an essential cognitive leap. The good news is that we're just emerging into a period of history when we can identify why we're continually torturing ourselves with unwanted emotions; blow the whistle on the root cause of our inner torment, confusion, and agitation; and then act to shift into more enjoyable, fulfilling realms of consciousness.

This book will spend just enough time on psychological and neurological discussions to make sure you understand the science behind our common dilemma, and the logical course of its resolution. But the ultimate aim isn't just to create a new intellectual concept. Instead, you're holding a hands-on manual that will teach you step-by-step psychological tools that can realistically liberate your mind from the grip of negative beliefs, thoughts, and emotions.

Some of these techniques have emerged from ancient meditative insights and practices, some from cutting-edge neurological and psychological research, some from far-out New Age experiments, and others from the more conservative realms of psychoanalysis, Gestalt and reality therapy, cognitive behavioral studies, and so on. Recent books, such as Antonio Damasio's *The Feeling of What Happens: Body and Emotion in the Making of Consciousness,* Judith Beck's *Cognitive Therapy: Basics and Beyond,* and John Welwood's *Toward a Psychology of Awakening,* have clearly elucidated specific academic dimensions of this progression toward a new vision of how the mind works and how we can act to become masters of our own inner destiny.

The introduction listed the dramatic changes that can be generated when we choose to quiet our overbusy thinking minds and open ourselves to new experience in the present moment. The positive effects of quieting our thoughts can also be readily seen through the personal experience of one of my recent clients.

Let's take a couple minutes to enjoy a short retelling of Richard's shift from no-choice to full-choice living. (Names and life details have been changed throughout to preserve anonymity.)

Richard Sees the Light

Richard's alarm clock went off with a loud jangle. Letting go of a vague dream, he blinked his eyes and woke up, his mind already starting, out of habit, to fixate on the most urgent challenges facing him that day. His wife woke up beside him with a welcoming smile, but instead of cuddling with her for a few moments, he sat up and began to mull over the details of a marketing presentation he had to deliver at 9:15 at the downtown office. Worried thoughts assaulted his mind as he realized he was still unsatisfied with some of the wording in his PowerPoint delivery.

Heading into the bathroom, Richard was already fully in problem-solving mode, his emotions tense and his body presence hardly acknowledged at all. Brushing his teeth, he found himself engaged in an imaginary argument with one of his coworkers, Oliver, defending his business logic and trying to come up with the exact words that would make Oliver look wrong at the meeting, rather than himself.

Twenty minutes later at the breakfast table, Richard had his laptop out making changes, fussing over details as he struggled to come up with some better wording for the first lines of his presentation. His teenage son came to the table wanting to talk about his tennis victory the day before, but Richard had no time for chatter – he was so consumed in his business worries that he barely focused on his son's presence at all. And when his wife put a comforting arm around him as he was heading out the door, he brushed aside her gesture – he was already gone in his mind and gave her no more than a perfunctory kiss as he hurried out to the car.

Driving downtown, Richard was impatient with traffic, and twice made half-conscious lane changes that could have caused an accident. Looking back suddenly at how heartlessly he'd acted with his family, he became swamped with guilt, worrying that he'd hurt his son's feelings and wondering if his wife would feel he didn't love her, even though he did very much.

He went into the office fast, still caught up in his family worries. When Oliver passed him in the hallway, Richard just scowled and then ignored him. They'd had a major run-in last week, and Richard was still angry at Oliver for resisting his new vision for the Lugombria account.

A few minutes later the meeting convened, with seven of Richard's superiors sitting around the table scowling at him as he tensely and somewhat aggressively gave his presentation, stumbling over some words and not really doing justice to his new ideas. And sure enough, Oliver attacked him right where he thought he would, and the ensuing argument made the whole meeting upsetting and indecisive.

Richard went stalking out of the building, driving back to his regional office feeling exhausted, angry, and fearful that he'd failed with his presentation. It seemed as though the whole world was down on him – he hated his work, hated Oliver, and could hardly manage to push forward with his life. He knew he was always doing his best, but somehow he remained a victim, caught up in worried feelings and paltry performance, over and over. As he drove out of the city he felt depressed, worried, angry, hopeless . . .

Richard's morning scenario seemed to be fated to happen, as if he were locked into a life loaded with anxiety, frustration, and guilt. But as we're learning in this book, he actually could have taken fate in his own hands at a number of crucial points and transformed his experience for the better. Let's take another look at Richard's morning, and identify the key choices he could have made to improve his business performance, and enhance his family experience as well.

Right when Richard wakes up, rather than letting his prevailing business worries immediately take over his mind, imagine how his morning would flow if he chooses to quiet his habitual thoughts and shift his attention toward the opportunity to snuggle for a few moments with his wife – thus beginning the day with heartfelt emotions and even a rush of sexual pleasure.

And while brushing his teeth, he again has the opportunity to put aside whatever thoughts about the future might come to mind, tuning instead into his physical body in the present moment, focusing on his breathing, his heartbeat, the feel of his bare feet on the cool tiles. As he walks downstairs, his mind clear and his body a pleasure to inhabit, he might have a sudden flash of business insight, seemingly out of the blue, suggesting a way to improve his PowerPoint presentation.

He takes his laptop to the breakfast table and makes his changes. Right in the middle of completing his notes, his son comes in. Richard chooses to let go of his work long enough to stand up and give the boy a fatherly hug, and chat with him about the tennis match. There's a flow of heartfelt love that feels good to both of them – then Richard dives back into his computer work as he finishes his breakfast.

He gives his wife a loving embrace before they both go out the door to their respective jobs. For just half a minute they let go of everything on their minds and experience the charge of intimacy that means so much to them both. As he leaves his home, he feels sharp in his mind, expansive in his heart, and in harmony with the world around him.

Driving through traffic, he's several times pulled into worrisome thoughts – but each time that he feels anxiety gripping his breathing, he makes the purposeful choice not to drift off into bothersome imaginings. Instead, he reflects upon several business moves he needs to make in the next couple of days, then does a special meditation he's learned to help awaken contact with his deeper sense of purpose in life.

By the time he's walking into the downtown office he's feeling confident of the outcome of the presentation, the people around him responding to his brightness with heartfelt greetings. When he meets his antagonist in the hallway, Richard doesn't react to him based on past experiences and judgments. Instead he smiles, opens his heart to the man – and even though Oliver doesn't completely let go of his own negative feelings, Richard can see that something softens between them.

The formal meeting and presentation unfold positively without any stress on Richard's part. He purposefully stays grounded in his body, calm and clear in his mind, accepting in his heart whatever might happen. Because he's not caught up in worries and power plays, his superiors admire his solid presence and receive his presentation with high praise. He even surprises himself with several flashes of spontaneous brilliance that emerge out of nowhere to make his presentation an obvious success. Meanwhile Oliver, rather than attacking him, realizes that the rest of the room supports Richard's proposal and there's no point in fighting.

Richard walks out of the building feeling like he did when he walked in. He wasn't anxious going in, and he's calm and satisfied as he goes out – taking a few minutes to chat with a colleague in the parking lot about mutual interests and making plans for a dinner that will be fun for all.

Realistic Progress

From experience, I can imagine what some of you are thinking right now. Sure, we've all heard these overbright scenarios promising to miraculously transform our lives through some simple trick that perhaps might work for some lucky people but probably won't work for us. Our lives aren't so simple, our worries aren't so facile, our mental habits aren't so easy to change. Obviously, if transforming our lives for the better were so easy, we'd all have done it already. Therefore, positive stories like the one we just heard don't necessarily inspire us. They sometimes even depress us because we feel that we're now being expected to instantly throw off a lifetime's worth of worrisome habits and mental fixations, as if it were no challenge at all.

As the author of this book and creator of experiential programs, I fully understand and appreciate such initial reactions. I'm well aware of the complexities and challenges facing each of us when we decide it's time to take more conscious control of our minds and develop the ability to refocus our attention in more positive directions.

At the same time, Richard's second story was not in any way a fairy-tale episode of unrealistic life improvement. Over the years my colleagues and I have observed a great many everyday people make major changes in their lives. At this point there's no question: When provided with effective experiential guidance and a clear conceptual understanding of the quiet-your-mind process, most people can indeed progress confidently toward the positive goals and results just described.

We're clearly not talking about a superficial fix that temporarily treats surface symptoms. We're talking about applying the most advanced techniques and working together over time to identify the core causes of an agitated, unsatisfied mind – and then step-by-step mastering these techniques so as to advance toward a more fulfilling and, let's say it, openly fun-filled approach to life.

Insights from Research

The psychiatrist and mind researcher Humphrey Osmond, like so many great scientists and humanitarians before him, has now receded into history, nearly forgotten by up-and-coming generations. But when I was just beginning my professional work in the late 1960s and 1970s, Dr. Osmond was recognized as one of the true bright lights in the psychological and medical research community. He was the wise yet supportive doctor in Aldous Huxley's classic autobiographical account of early psychedelic research, *The Doors of Perception.* For over two decades he served as both leader and mentor of the new research community that was struggling to make scientific sense of the often radical insights of professionals who were exploring the psychological and neurological effects of physical and cognitive stress, emotional trauma, hypnosis, alcohol, marijuana, and psychedelics and the expanding frontiers of human consciousness.

I considered myself lucky to be offered the position of research hypnotist at Humphrey Osmond's Bureau of Research in Neurology and Psychiatry at the New Jersey Neuro-Psychiatric Institute. For our present discussion I want to mention the seminal months during which Dr. Osmond oversaw our research into how the brain's performance might be altered when a subject's conscious attention shifts from deductive thinking to pure present-moment sensory experience. The results of these studies forever impacted my understanding of the primary ways in which we can liberate ourselves from the grip of our own noisy mental chatter and shift into present-moment engagement with the world around us.

The research protocol was straightforward: Each of our thirty-two subjects read a biology text for five minutes, then put the book aside and focused their attention fully on various sensory inputs, such as the sensation of the air flowing in and out the nose, the sensation of chest and belly movements while breathing, the sensation of heartbeat or pulse, the sensation of auditory inputs (sounds) and visual inputs (selected objects), and so forth. The subjects were wired to EEG (electroencephalographic) equipment and to machines measuring changes in heart rate, blood pressure, body temperature, and so forth. We also conducted special pre- and post-interviews for data on subjective experience.

What we found was that, statistically, both subjective and objective indicators showed definite changes in brain activity, bodily functioning, and inner emotional experience, demonstrating experimentally – perhaps for the first time – that the simple act of shifting one's mental focus from thinking to experiencing does indeed change one's basic neurological and physiological functioning.

Under Dr. Osmond's guidance we then took the next logical research step, that of purposefully shifting the subject's focus from a negative thought (worrying about a topic of anxious concern for the subject) to a present-moment "sensation focus" on such sensory inputs as breathing, sounds, enjoyable sights, and so forth. Again we found that definite changes in brain activity and bodily function were elicited, only in this case (with the introduction of the emotion of anxiety) there were dramatically greater changes than before.

Then we again placed subjects in a worried state of mind, and tested to see if there was any difference when they focused on one or two perceptual inputs (breathing, a sound, a sight) at the same time. As predicted from the meditation studies of staff member Alan Watts, we found that focusing on just one perceptual input failed to immediately shift the subject fully out of worried thoughts into experiencing the present moment, but when the subject focused on two or more sensory inputs at the same time, there were immediate shifts in brainwave activity, as well as the subjective experience of reduced anxiety. Indeed, in several similar experiments, we discovered that it is very difficult or even impossible to think clearly with deductive mentation while also focusing on two or more sensory inputs – the perceptual activity by and large short-circuits the thinking process.

This chapter is dedicated to the insights that emerged from such early research, insights now clearly confirmed by the new brain-mapping technologies which allow us to photograph quite dramatically how different parts of the brain light up or quiet down when the subject shifts from cognitive to sensory fixations, and from one emotion to another. The next time you're in a bookstore or library you might want to go to the psychology section and look at the actual color images of this research in books such as *Brain Mapping* by Arthur Toga and *Mapping the Mind: Secrets of the Human Brain* by Joel Davis.

There is no longer any question about the physiological and neurological impact of a shift in mental focus and activity, and resulting changes in brain functioning and bodily condition. Specifically, as we've just seen, when we turn our attention away from our thought-flows, whatever they might be, toward two or more sensory inputs at the same time, thoughts simply stop flowing through our minds. This is obviously a primary key to quieting the mind, and something you can do at any time or place to stop bothersome thoughts and tune into the present moment.

Practice Makes Perfect

Let's take a few moments to explore your ability to observe your own thoughts as they flow through your mind . . . and then perhaps to shift your attention away from thinking and toward the experience coming to you right now in this present moment.

Don't be discouraged if, at first, you find that you have difficulty in holding your full attention to your immediate sensory inputs. Your mind almost surely has developed an ingrained reflex that tends to pull you back into thinking mode, for reasons we'll explore in depth later on. If so, just notice this habit, observe it in action – and regularly practice this simple yet effective focusing exercise until you begin to master the ability to shift from cognitive to perceptual fixation at will. At the end of this chapter I'll present a formal training session, with accompanying online audio guidance, to make sure you master this elementary but essential mental shifting process. In the meantime, try this exercise.

PAUSE AND EXPERIENCE

•

After reading this paragraph, if you like, choose to put the book aside for a couple minutes, close your eyes, and gently turn your mind toward the actual physical sensation of the air flowing in and out your nose as you breathe. At the same time, be aware of the movements in your chest and belly as you breathe . . . and at the same time, be aware of any sounds around you as you continue breathing . . . and notice how your mind has become more quiet. . . .

Essential Brain Talk

The exercise you just performed demonstrates how you can prove on your own, from the inside out, what we discovered in the lab years ago: that conscious perceptual shifts can change your inner experience. Let's now look a bit deeper into how your mind actually functions to generate this shift in experience. Please bear with me for a few pages as I explain how your brain functions, as this overview will serve us well in later discussions.

As I'm sure you know, our human brains are phenomenally complex. In some ways we share many characteristics with the most lowly of life forms on this planet, through regions of our brains that operate almost entirely on preprogrammed hardwired formats designed to maintain basic bodily functioning and safety. Indeed, it was recently discovered that over 97 percent of our DNA is identical to that of a field mouse. The structure of our brains hasn't changed noticeably in over 20,000 years, which means we're basically employing the same neurological system that we did when we were primitive hunter-gatherers. This explains in part why many of our emotional reactions to situations seem outdated and in many cases, seriously counterproductive to our contemporary well-being.

At the opposite end of the consciousness spectrum, we also possess uniquely human qualities of expanded mental performance and experience – including a vast capacity for rational thought, emotional empathy, intuitive insight – enabling us to perform amazing technological feats and intellectual acrobatics, and even perhaps to transcend personal consciousness altogether and move into transpersonal realms of shared consciousness.

As each new day of our lives unfolds, we are continually shifting from one type of brain function to another. Sometimes we find our minds fixated perceptually upon pure bodily sensations; sometimes our limbic system grabs us with intense emotional reactions; at other times we get totally lost in abstract thought and problem solving; often we become consumed in social intercourse that holds us focused in the present moment, while at other times we're completely gone from the world around us, busy recalling the past or imagining the future. And as mentioned above, rarely but significantly by a still-mysterious process of whole-brain mental integration, we experience flashes of remarkable intuitive insight, and even a deep sense of mystic oneness and total spiritual transcendence.

How can we have so many quite distinct types of experience within one brain? The answer, as I'm sure you know from all the recent media discussions about the brain, is that we possess several quite distinct evolutionary layers of brain systems inside our heads, each with particular capabilities and responsibilities and all interacting with each other. There has recently been far too much simplistic generalization about the roles and interactions of the different regions of our brains. However, while remaining true to the remarkable complexity and interactivity of our brains, we can make several basic observations that will help us in our discussions. If this is known ground for you, of course, just skip quickly through this section.

Key to our present discussion, the left hemisphere of the cerebral cortex, as documented by recent innovations in brain-scan technologies, does appear to be the primary seat of deductive, logical, linear thinking. This part of the brain is masterful in analyzing and categorizing, in judging and problem solving, in manipulating symbols and generating meaningful thoughts. This is where our ingrained beliefs interact with what we're choosing to do in life, and our sense of right and wrong comes into conscious expression.

In contemporary society, with our chronic fixation upon deductive thinking as opposed to intuitive reflection, left-brain activity tends to dominate our conscious minds most of the time. To the extent that linear logical thinking, grounded in our basic beliefs and assumptions about life, determines what we do, it's this ever-busy thought-based "ego" dimension of the brain that's in charge.

A key psychological feature of the left hemisphere is that in most brains, it is within this region that we perceive the flow of time as a linear past-future phenomenon. Within this general model, this hemisphere takes symbolic information and mental assumptions developed from past experience and uses this information to analyze current life events in order to create new concepts, assumptions, and beliefs, and also to project into the future and make plans to control our lives, hopefully in a positive direction.

The capacity of the logical thinking mind, the seat of the ego, to assume a certain amount of control over our lives can be very helpful – when regularly moderated and balanced by our intuitive, experiential, and spiritual dimensions. But all too often the deductive mind tends to become a "control freak" that rules rigidly by preconceived fear-based expectations and beliefs – leaving little or no room for spontaneity and playful action motivated by the heart and soul. Furthermore, as we've seen, our thoughts almost always stimulate emotional responses in our bodies, and when our thoughts are fear-based, our emotions are going to be no fun at all.

Luckily for our full experience of life, we're not just rational thinking machines generating emotional reactions. We also have several other vital functions of our minds that interact with our thinking, to generate more insightful and spontaneous flows of thoughts through our minds – and also to deliver experience beyond all thought, when our thinking minds become quiet and other realms of consciousness emerge. The right hemisphere of the cerebral cortex, for instance, is capable of remarkable nonlinear intuitive dimensions of consciousness, providing us with our spontaneous sense of present-moment awareness and with the experience of harmony, compassion, beauty, and integration.

In direct contrast to the point-by-point linear function of the left hemisphere, the right hemisphere tends to perceive the whole at once, rather than to fixate upon a part of the whole. It's through this ability to perceive the whole at once (actually shown in brain-scanning images as many areas of the brain operating at once) that our sudden and often invaluable flashes of insight appear to come into existence, far beyond the confines of regular linear mentation.

The memory-based thoughts, expectations, and assumptions of left-brain thought-flows are often quite enjoyable, and in the case of problem solving, downright essential on a fairly regular basis. However, memory-based deductive thoughts and images are also primarily responsible for stimulating such negative emotions as anxiety, shame, anger, and depression. In contrast, the more present-moment experiential mode of our right brain is associated with generating the positive "thoughtless" feelings of compassion, joy, pleasure, well-being, and bliss.

Indeed, as brain scans of meditators have recently documented, a shift from high left-brain activity to high right-brain activity is directly correlated with a shift from mundane thinking to spiritual/meditative experience.

Mind management involves primarily the fine art of choosing wisely, and regularly, where to hold our mind's focus of attention – because all else emerges from that primary choice and decision. Again, let's practice what we preach and take time to actually experience what we're talking about.

PAUSE AND EXPERIENCE
•

You are presently engaged in reading this logical flow of symbols, clearly a left-brain deductive function of the mind. After reading this paragraph, see what experience comes to you that might be of a more intuitive or even spiritual nature, as you put the book aside and again tune into your breathing experience . . . and at the same time, your heart . . . the sounds all around you . . . what your eyes see as you look around the room . . . and as you experience from the inside out your brain shifting its functioning, be open to a new experience. . . .

The Experience Portal

Along with what we refer to as the left and right sides of the cerebral cortex, we also have two other primary regions of the brain that are vital to our present discussions: the limbic area of the emotional-associational brain, and the various regions of the perceptual brain. The limbic region, from whence both our emotions and our memories emerge, lies directly under the cerebral cortex and is intimately involved in the workings of both hemispheres. In less complex creatures with no capacity for rational thought, the limbic system, in conjunction with a perceptual instant-analysis system called the "primitive fear center" or amygdala, responds directly to present-moment happenings to provoke bodily fight-or-flight action.

However, in our more complex human brains, instead of present-moment perceptions and emotional and physiological responses provoking present-moment behavior, it's just the other way around. As we're learning step-by-step, our chronic thoughts (memories of the past, judgments of the present, imaginations of the future) tend to be the primary source of our resulting emotions and actions.

It's vital to see to the core of the human brain's unique capacity to generate thoughts and images, memories and imaginations, that in turn provoke an emotional response, that in turn provoke bodily feelings and behavior – even in the complete absence of any real-world present-moment provocations. A great majority of human suffering is caused by this vicious mental circuit where habitual worrisome thoughts provoke anxious feelings and behavior, and these anxious bodily feelings in turn provoke more worrisome thoughts, ad infinitum in a generally anxious person – unless the circuit is somehow consciously broken by shifting the focus of attention to the fourth primary function of the mind – that of present-moment sensation and perception centered in the lower middle of the brain called the diencephalon.

From the point of view of this discussion, certainly one of the most striking discoveries about the functioning of the human mind is that in order to enter into "higher" states of integrated consciousness, we must first shift our attention to the most ancient part of our mind, the physical sensory realm of immediate perception. Shifting from deductive into perceptual awareness, as I'm teaching you to do in this chapter, seems to be like putting in the clutch in order to shift gears; the shift to sensory awareness quiets the usual chatter of the mind so that a deeper intuitive experience can emerge.

Your Interior Commentator

If there's so much to be gained by making this cognitive shift away from left-brain deductive activity toward what is often a more enjoyable sensory, intuitive, and spiritual realm of consciousness, why do we tend to remain stuck in deductive thinking so much of the time? What is it that keeps our thinking minds constantly busy? Where's all the chatter that fills our inner ears actually coming from?

Each human being on this planet, like it or not, possesses (or is possessed by) a very talkative inner voice, an "interior commentator" that almost constantly dominates the consciousness show. This ego function of the mind is chronically busy analyzing everything we encounter as we go through our day, making ongoing comments and judgments about what we might be encountering.

As I'm sure you've noticed from the inside out, this sometimes whispering, sometimes loud inner voice represents the

majority of all our mental activity during the day. Our interior commentator chatters almost constantly. Sometimes, if
we're lucky, our interior commentator is inspired by a deeper
wisdom, drawing inspiration from not only the deductive but
also the intuitive realms of consciousness. But all too often, the
inner voice is caught up in worried or stressed-out or judgmental fear-based thoughts that generate an underlying fight-
flight fear response inside us.

But here's the curious thing about our ego voice: It truly
believes that we couldn't possibly manage to get through the
day without its constant help. And for complex reasons that
I'd need a whole book to clarify, we human beings in general
have so strongly identified with this reflective, judging part
of our mind that we automatically accept the presence of the
voice.

What's the reality orient? As long as our ego voice is busy
judging and evaluating and ruminating about everything that
appears before us, it's very difficult for us to have any meaningful direct heart-to-heart encounter with the outside world,
or to tune into our deeper feelings and intuitive insights that
might otherwise rise to the fore and be of great value to us.

However, for a great many of us, our inner commentator
possesses a saving grace – a capacity to shift beyond fear-based
judgments and integrate its defensive stance with a more expansive, love-based quality. After all, who is allowing you to
read this book right now, if not your inner commentator? Obviously the ego voice is often not completely out of hand at all,
but rather doing its best, with all its various compulsions and
apprehensions, to make choices that will serve the greater
good of your organism.

How do you know if the decisions of your own inner commentator are reliable? Ask yourself this question: At any given moment, is that voice operating out of fear or out of love? This is the key indicator of whether the ego voice can be trusted.

At any time you can step back and listen to the content of your inner voice and observe the logic (based on fear or not) being applied to a decision. When your inner voice is habitually anxious it tends to constantly think worried thoughts, and these fearful thoughts in turn, as we saw earlier, generate fearful emotions, choices, and actions – which tend to lead to more fearful thoughts, leading deeper and deeper into anxious, weak, reactionary behavior and experiences.

But when your interior commentator doesn't feel worried, when love and trust and joy dominate the content of your thoughts, then your thoughts will be creative and a pleasure.

Your inner commentator's willingness to explore the ideas and techniques in this book is a solid indicator. It shows that your cognitive ego presence, although of course sometimes caught up in worrisome thoughts and bothersome thought-flows, is already tapped into a wisdom that can hear the value of what we're talking about, and consider risking the ultimate leap of faith – that of letting go of ego control and learning how to participate in a greater conscious whole.

What About the Bad Things

I've been lauding the perceptual and intuitive present moment as the optimum place to hold one's focus of attention, because "here and now" is where life truly unfolds moment to moment. Yet as we all know from experience, the present moment isn't always such a bright rosy place to be. Sure, all the good things that happen to us do happen only in the here and now. But all the bad things also happen to us only in the present moment.

From a logical point of view, if the here and now is the only place where we can get hit with negative experiences, maybe it makes excellent sense to avoid being so intimately and vulnerably tuned into the present moment all the time. Maybe it makes more sense to do what in fact most of us do with our lives, and avoid the direct negative blasts that can hit us from the present moment – by staying mostly in the seemingly safe past-future dimensions of the thinking mind.

This is a very important point that is too often ignored, glossed over, and otherwise perennially misunderstood. Yes, bad things do happen to us in the present moment – the here and now is the backdrop upon which all of life plays itself out moment by moment. We receive new blows from the outside world, not in the past or the future realms of the thinking mind but right here in the present realm of the experiential mind.

However, consider the following. How many minutes of each new day of your life would you say are overtly negative, causing you intense emotional or physical pain or discomfort through new incoming experience? This question doesn't include all the emotional and resultant physical suffering that gets provoked by your inner mind's ability to fixate on negative thoughts and worrying. We're talking about the percentage of your actual experiential day that hits you with a decidedly negative encounter in the here and now.

The truth is, this experiential world of our contemporary society is by and large, remarkably benign. Most of the time we're not subjected to extremes of temperature in our homes and workplaces; people aren't attacking us and hurting us;

most of the time we're with friendly folk rather than antagonistic people; we eat comparatively great food; we have many opportunities to gaze at something beautiful if we take the time; we can listen to excellent music suited to our tastes; and we can move our bodies and in general feel good inside our own skins, stretching when we want to most of the time.

In sum, the outside experiential world that we tune into when we quiet our minds and focus on what our bodies are experiencing in the moment, is mostly a positive experience for us to enjoy, not a negative experience to avoid.

Furthermore, when something negative does happen in the world around us, surely we do best to be fully conscious in the here and now, so that we can spontaneously respond to the challenging situation. When we're lost in thought and something bad happens around us, we can snap into the present moment to deal with it. So it seems that upon logical analysis, the idea of avoiding the present moment because bad things sometimes happen here just doesn't hold up.

In fact, most of our chronic torments emerge not from right here and now, but from our thinking minds dwelling on bad things that happened in the past to us, or imagining something anxiety-provoking that might happen sometime in the future. The present moment is quite clearly our God-given haven from all such mentally generated suffering.

Even though I just presented a logical case for not being afraid of the present moment, still I know from therapy work that many of you are carrying old beliefs at subliminal levels, that make you habitually shy away from spending time in the present moment. Perhaps you feel bored with the present moment, so that the boredom pushes you back into thought. Perhaps you actually feel a tinge of apprehension when you shift into the present moment, and that apprehension pops you back into thought. Who knows what defense mechanism you built, supposedly to keep yourself safe, by avoiding the present moment. The next two chapters will specifically help you identify such outdated fears and show you how to let go of them.

Thinking and Experiencing Together

We've been talking a lot about quieting the habitual thinking mind so that new experiences can emerge. But does this mean we must give up thinking altogether, in order to be fully here? There's been much talk about the separation of the left and right hemispheres of the cerebral cortex, and indeed, most of the time it seems that we function mostly on an either-or basis of deduction-cognition or sensation-intuition.

However, it's now high time to talk about the neurological fact that the left and right hemispheres do have distinct functions – yet they are also strongly connected by a part of the brain called the corpus callosum. This remarkable and little-understood connective system contains over 200 million tiny fibers, each of which can fire up to 1,000 times a second – which implies a potential for communication and cooperation between left and right hemispheres that's really quite staggering.

Indeed, exploratory brain scans of different mental functions and emotional states indicate that when we're engaged in special creative mental activity that is strongly influenced by insights and sudden flashes of new ideas, both hemispheres are firing off together or dominance is shifting rapidly from one hemisphere to the other. Thus, even though we usually consider "thinking" and "experiencing" as quite distinct and separate, we do possess the potential neurological capacity to merge the two into one greater consciousness.

And for me, this indeed is what consciousness expansion is all about – learning to let go of habitual limiting mental fixations so as to become aware of a greater whole, wherein our minds function at much higher levels of integrated performance. We're going to progress step-by-step toward this goal in these programs, to the point where you can quiet your mundane thinking mind at will, be purely in the present moment – and then in that expanded moment, right in the middle of perceiving the intuitive whole of a situation, allow a new type of thought to begin to flow, as the corpus callosum integrates left and right into a greater whole.

The beautiful psychological fact is this: When you quiet your habitual chattering ego thoughts and tune your attention into heart-felt sensory experience, and then open up to an integrative experience of "everything at once," thoughts often do indeed begin to flow again. But here's the difference – these new thought-flows, emerging directly out of the here and now and coming into being while you're deeply in touch with your heart and soul, will be of an entirely different quality than those that emerge semiautomatically from your conditioned past.

Why? Because worrying thoughts have been silenced in the shift into present-moment perceptual awareness. Therefore these new thoughts will come into being without anxiety or other negative emotions polluting them, as a result of an integration of your intuitive and higher deductive capabilities. In essence, this is what insight is all about – this is how we suddenly find ourselves thinking inspired thoughts. We've quieted the chronic thoughts of our deductive mind, we've entered into a higher state of consciousness where spirit or higher wisdom can impact our personal lives – and in this expansive state of mind, we experience a spontaneous flow of thoughts inspired by our perception of the whole at once.

With this understanding, it's obvious that in our quiet-your-mind process the inner commentator is not being shut out of the picture, but rather is being offered the remarkable opportunity to tap into a deeper level of inspiration for its flow of thoughts through the mind.

The truth is, we can all readily aspire to living our lives constantly in a higher level of consciousness, as our interior commentator learns to stop thinking fearful thoughts, learns how to be quiet and await the flow of inspired thoughts. Nothing except our ingrained mental habits keep us from being in this expansive state right now.

Seen from a broad perspective, as a species we seem to be engaged in the evolutionary unfolding of a remarkable mental potential. For most people until now, that potential has been limited by the overdominance of one dimension of consciousness – fear-based cognitive mentation. Now we seem to be in the process of consciously choosing to expand into more integrative realms of consciousness that spiritual masters have explored for many millennia, and which are now rising up to become every person's birthright.

The key to this transformation of our daily experience of life is to be found in how we employ the ultimate power we all possess, which we are just now learning to consciously direct in radically empowering ways.

Quieting Your Mind

Without further ado, let us begin to master the most effective and fastest way to quiet your thoughts, and thus open up to the rest of your mind's experiential potential. You'll want to practice moving through this process a number of times over the next days and weeks, until the shifting process becomes second nature, holding in mind that practice makes perfect, that you're not expected to master the shifting process the first time, and that this entire book and set of audio programs is dedicated to making sure that you do master the process.

The guided experience you're now going to explore is so basic that you'll find it at the end of the first chapter of most of my books. There's simply no other place to begin, except here. The four-step process takes just a minute or two to do, and will always make you feel immediately better inside your own skin, so you'll naturally want to incorporate it into your schedule a number of times each day.

You'll also find as you read deeper into this book that all the more advanced programs you'll be learning require that you first move through this initial cognitive-shifting process, to advance your focus of attention into position for exploring the various specific programs being taught.

You can either read through the process printed below and memorize the steps so that you can guide yourself through the process, or have a friend guide you through the experience, or go to my website and let me guide you through the process via streamed audio or download.

You've learned in this chapter that by focusing on two or more distinct sensations, you can instantly quiet all thoughts and enter into a more peaceful state of being in the present moment. The following process focuses your attention purposefully on the two always-present sources of bodily sensation that sustain your moment-to-moment being. Thus you accomplish two major goals with one process: You bring your awareness fully away from past-future mental ruminations and worries into the present moment; and you directly perceive from the inside out your moment-to-moment core bodily activities that keep you alive. So now, let's do it!

GUIDED SESSION 1:

QUIETING YOUR THOUGHTS

•

For the next few minutes, just make sure you're comfortable . . . go ahead and stretch a little if you want . . . yawn maybe . . . and without any effort or judgment, observe whatever's happening in your mind right now.

Where is your focus of attention? Is your thinking mind quiet, or are there thoughts regularly popping into mind? . . . Just watch them coming and going. . . .

Now let's gently begin to shift your mind's focus of attention away from thinking about life, toward the actual experience of life happening right here, right now.

Begin to turn your mind's focus of attention, toward the actual sensation of the air flowing in and out, through your nose or mouth . . . make no effort to inhale, or exhale . . . let your breathing stop when it wants to . . . and start when it wants to . . . and feel the air as it comes flowing in . . . flowing out . . . set your breathing free . . .

While you remain aware of the air flowing in and out your nose or mouth, expand your awareness to also include the sensations of movement happening in your chest and belly, as you breathe . . .

While you remain aware of the air flowing in and out your nose or mouth . . . and the movements in your chest and belly as you breathe . . . expand your awareness to also include your heart, beating right in the middle of your breathing . . .

Be aware of your whole body at once, here in this present moment . . .

Your thoughts are now quiet . . . your attention fully here in the present moment . . . and as you enjoy this peace and quiet, stay aware of your breathing . . . your heart . . . observe whatever happens in your mind, without judgment . . . and be open to new perceptions, and insights . . .

For streamed-audio guidance through this experience, go to www.johnselby.com.

chapter 2

quieting judgmental thoughts

Many of you probably had reasonable if temporary success in quieting your mind and shifting your focus of attention to your own presence in the here and now. As mentioned earlier, practice will make perfect, and I encourage you to regularly pause and move through this basic shifting technique until you master it.

However, in the beginning, this mental-shifting process alone probably won't be adequate for most of you in breaking entirely free from your mind's thinkaholic habits. Yes, you'll gain a few moments of peace and quiet inside your own mind every time you do the breathing, heart, whole-body meditation, and this in itself can prove a godsend. But all too soon you'll find yourself swept back into a flow of thoughts, which will in turn generate feelings of uncertainty, apprehension, self-doubt, irritation, guilt, and all the rest.

In this chapter we're going to go the next step in this quiet-mind process, as we look to the very source of human suffering and dis-ease – the dominant tendency of our minds to be chronically locked in heartless, fear-based, judgment mode, rather than in loving-acceptance, pure-enjoyment mode. We're going to explore your mind's natural tendency to be almost constantly judging everything it encounters – and in that basic act of judging, generating separation between you and your heart, you and the world around you, you and your own deeper intuitive and spiritual presence.

Again let's use an example from one of my clients, to show in action how the judgmental function of the human mind generates discord and anxiety, and how the programs being learned in this book can effectively shift your focus of attention beyond such detrimental judgment habits.

Judge Not . . .

Nicole hurried home from work feeling upset with herself. Not once in the seven months since her breakup with Gerald, had she met a new person who thrilled her – until she met Michael at a party last weekend. This morning he'd phoned out of the blue and asked her over to his home tonight for dinner, and for some reason she'd been an utter fool (or so she scolded herself) and said yes. Now her critical mind was full of reasons why he couldn't possibly be the ideal man she was looking for – he wasn't quite tall enough to suit her, he was too cocksure of himself, he had been a subtle flirt at the party. . . .

As she let herself into her apartment, she caught her mind conjuring up all sorts of embarrassing or even downright emotionally threatening scenarios that might happen during dinner – and especially afterward if they continued further into the evening together. "The guy's so pushy," she told herself, "too dominating – he just isn't my type. Besides, he'd probably realize I'm not sexy enough for him, or smart enough."

Nicole was 27 and already doing very well in her profession, but like many people, she was still having difficulties with personal worries and negative attitudes that all too often got in her way socially. For several months now, she'd been working with her therapist (whom she referred to as her personal trainer) to master a new approach for breaking free of outdated beliefs and anxious feelings that assailed her, especially in intimate situations. She'd now learned how *not* to fall victim to old dating anxieties and self-judgments, for example. So, making herself comfortable on the sofa, she spent a few moments observing her scattered mental condition, then took active control of the situation. She purposefully turned her focus of attention away from her compulsive thoughts and imaginings, toward an acute perceptual awareness of her own physical presence . . . her breaths coming and going . . . her heartbeat . . . her whole-body experience here and now . . .

A short time later she completed the "calming the mind" process she'd been practicing for several weeks now. Opening her eyes, she was pleased to note that she was feeling better, more grounded and tuned into the world around her – but still, right on the edge of her consciousness she could feel all the old dating apprehensions just waiting to pounce on her. So she moved into the next step of the mental process she'd recently learned. She turned her attention directly toward the shaky feelings and nervous emotions inside her body and consciously allowed herself to verbalize those mostly unspoken assumptions and beliefs that were chronically undermining her otherwise fulfilling life.

The first thought that she discovered right under the surface of her negative emotions about the coming evening, was a surprisingly angry thought: "Michael's so full of himself, he's obviously an egotistic jerk, he's not at all good enough for me. I should phone him right now and cancel the dinner."

The chance to escape from the anxiety of the dinner date was seductive, but rather than indulging in this runaway behavior, Nicole calmly asked herself the key question: "Now wait a minute, is that negative thought about Michael really true? How do I know he's a jerk? Am I just projecting the judgment onto him out of fear?"

When she honestly looked at this question, Nicole realized that her negative attitude toward Michael – mostly unconsciously – didn't hold up under close scrutiny. In fact, from her experience of him thus far, deep down she considered Michael the exact opposite of a jerk. He was handsome, gentlemanly, and intelligent, and the look in his eyes had been so gentle, so encouraging . . .

As she admitted this to herself, she found another, even deeper negative judgment suddenly surfacing. "It's me who's the jerk, not him. And as soon as he gets to know me a little better tonight, he'll reject me – because I've got so many problems, I'm a wreck inside, and I'm definitely not good enough for someone like him."

Nicole had recently admitted to her therapist that she harbored an underlying feeling that she was "not being good enough." But this time, instead of getting depressed by the thought, she employed her newfound ability to rationally evaluate this belief. As she was learning in therapy, she was entirely fed up with all her negative self-attitudes and beliefs, which were chronically dragging her down. She was clear in her mind that what she wanted more than anything was to

stop judging herself and learn to accept and love herself just
as she was.

All things considered, she knew she was more than good
enough to be with Michael without being judged by him. She
wasn't perfect, and her last relationship had gone down in
flames – but she was learning and growing and she had a lot
of love to give. She reminded herself that what she wanted
from a new relationship was compassion and understanding,
not further judgment. If Michael couldn't deliver that basic
feeling of heartfelt acceptance, then he simply wasn't the right
man for her.

So she made a pact with herself. This evening she wasn't
going to judge either her date or herself at all. Instead, she
was going to do an experiment. She was going to trust the
wisdom and direct response of her heart, rather than the analysis of her judging mind – and she was going to expect Michael
do the same. Otherwise, there was no hope of any true love
blossoming at all.

Feeling much better about herself and the evening, Nicole
jumped up, took a quick shower, put on a simple dress rather
than trying to impress Michael with clothes, and headed on
her way into her new adventure. "Whatever happens with
Michael," she told herself as she went downstairs for a cab, "I
feel good about myself." She admitted that yes, she was still
some distance from fully breaking free of childhood beliefs
about being inadequate – but just saying those positive words
worked a bit of magic.

Arriving at Michael's, she felt ready and eager for whatever
might come this evening. The moon had broken through the
clouds overhead, and as she crossed the street she actually ran
a bit, feeling light on her toes and good in her body, ready for

whatever might come. She noticed her mind starting to evaluate the neighborhood that Michael lived in (a positive judgment because it was a very enjoyable neighborhood, but a judgment all the same), and she chose to let the judging thoughts go before they could influence her deeper feelings for the man.

As she stood at Michael's door waiting for him to answer the bell, again she got hit with those terrible nervous shakes and insecurities that had so often plagued her romantic life. But now she knew what to do. She purposefully shifted her mind's present focus away from her apprehensive thoughts and anticipations and instead, concentrated her full attention on the vital sensory feelings of being alive right now in her body, her feet solid against the floor, her heart excited . . .

The door opened and there he was, his eyes bright but also a little uncertain. For a moment they both stood there unmoving. She could see he was just as nervous as she was – and they both seemed to arrive at that realization at the same time, because they burst out laughing at their mutual shyness. The social ice was immediately broken, and that natural intimacy they'd felt at the party last week was still alive.

She walked into his home, not judging his interior decorating skills – not judging anything at all, in fact – just being there with him in the present moment. She smelled the dinner he'd cooked for her, sighed with relief at having passed successfully through that difficult romantic portal, and accepted a glass of white wine. Her emotions were unusually calm, her senses acutely aware of everything that was unfolding in their shared experience of this exciting new moment together.

Observing Without Judging

Nicole's personal experience, as she related it to me the next day, highlights the prime value of learning to identify and quiet judgmental thoughts that otherwise can make a stressful muddle of so many situations we find ourselves in. Judge not . . .

"But wait," your logical mind might reasonably object, "surely we need to discriminate between green and red at the traffic light? Surely we need to judge whether it's safe to cross the street? And isn't it wise to judge the people we encounter in the park as potentially dangerous and best to avoid? Logic dictates that constantly judging the world around us is our best way of keeping ourselves safe and thriving."

Good point. All esoteric notions aside, can we really get by in life by leading with our hearts rather than our judging minds? Was Nicole being a fool to trust the present moment to unfold successfully without constantly judging what's happening, or had she entered a highly successful path by employing the fine art of nonjudgmental relating? Is it really possible to participate in the world in a mostly nonjudgmental way, living our lives free from past-programmed attitudes and beliefs?

Let me share with you a scientific, neurological answer to this question so that we begin with the most basic understanding of how our brains automatically protect us from danger, even when our thinking minds are entirely quiet.

As we move through each new moment, regardless of what we're doing or how we're directing our conscious attention, a particular ancient region of our brain called the diencephalon is in fact busy taking care of us. It's constantly working, even when we're sleeping, making sure that nothing harms us in any way. Each and every perceptual input being received by our brain from the outside world, be it visual, auditory, tactile, olfactory, or kinesthetic, goes first to the diencephalon and is then routed to a nearby region of the limbic system called the amygdala – the early warning system of our brain.

Located deep within our emotion-memory-association center, the amygdala, consisting of two almond-sized clusters of brain cell bundles, receives each and every perceptual input we experience and screens it to make sure it contains no information that might be associated with danger. In less than one-tenth of a second the amygdala processes each perceptual input, and if it comes across a perception associated with danger, it pushes the red-alert button of the brain – the fear button. This amygdala region is rightfully called the "primitive fear system." It is what enables us to instantly shift into action mode to deal with a danger without any intervening thought. It makes us react to loud noises, to the danger of falling of a cliff, to anything crawling on our skin, to sudden movements in the periphery of our vision, to the presence of a potentially venomous snake or spider. All animals have a type of amygdala. It's been in active development for many millions of evolutionary years, and is essential to the very survival of every living creature on the planet.

The amygdala, in conjunction with other related memory and association functions of the mind, is not only hardwired with fear indicators, it is also constantly learning about new dangers through experience and developing an ever more sensitive process for screening perceptual inputs for potential dangers. It's the ideal self-updating, self-operating early warning system. Even when your mind is quiet of judgmental thoughts, the amygdala has the power to instantly pull your attention away from whatever you're consciously focusing on and direct your full attention toward dealing with a perceived danger. Rest assured that, even with your conscious judgmental thinking mind fully at rest, the amygdala region of your brain is constantly monitoring your environment, ready to alert you if there's any danger to deal with. When it sees a red light across the street, for instance, in one-tenth of a second it shifts your conscious focus of attention to dealing with the possible danger from oncoming traffic.

Now, here's where being human is different from being a dog or a cat or an elephant or a bat. As we will explore in more depth in Chapter 3, the human mind has the unique ability to halt the initial fight-or-flight reaction triggered by the primitive fear center, long enough to consciously analyze the present situation through the process of cognitive deduction – to make sure there's a danger really present, before reacting with fear.

In the frontal lobes of the cerebral cortex we possess the "rational fear system" that responds to the primitive fear system's initial alert signal, and quickly thinks through the available perceptual information at hand, in order to come to a logical conclusion regarding the reality of the situation. If you suddenly see a red light across the street, you go on instant alert to a possible danger, and then usually you take a second or two of rapid rational analysis of the situation to decide whether to stop or cross the street anyway.

Subtle Judgments

This all sounds reasonable and good. But even if you know and accept that your amygdala is looking out for perceptual red flags, very probably the idea of living spontaneously in the present moment, without your mind constantly evaluating, judging, and manipulating what you're experiencing, might still run seriously contrary to your ingrained notions of how life is supposed to be. You've almost certainly been programmed since you were very young to constantly evaluate everything that you encounter in life, not only as dangerous or safe but also as either good for you or bad, enjoyable or a bother, positive or negative, right or wrong, helpful or detrimental, something to try to acquire or something to avoid. Don't you need to keep this higher-level judgmental action happening in your mind to make sure nothing bad happens to you?

It is true that the very nature of our cognitive mind is to compare and contrast, to evaluate and associate. And surely it's important to our survival to regularly pause and consciously, quite beyond the primitive fear system's level of discernment, evaluate our situation – to make decisions and plans based on our best rational analysis. After all, that's how human beings have come out on top.

Yet spiritual masters such as Jesus and Buddha, Mohammed and Lao Tzu, have said very clearly in their own way, "Judge not, or you will be judged." This statement is one of the most insightful psychological observations about how the human mind works. When you look to the core of the judgment phenomenon, you will see quite clearly that if you go around continually judging everything you encounter, you're naturally going to end up totally caught up in judgment mode, and thus shut out from the more spiritual, heart-centered realms of a truly fulfilling life.

Yes, we do need to discriminate and evaluate our posture in certain situations. The key point being made in this book is that judgmental cognitive activity is best used only when it is absolutely required. At all other times, make sure the mind's judgment mode is in the "off" or "on hold" position

Why? Because while our minds are busy judging a situation, we're mostly lost to the present moment as we compare
the present situation with all associated experiences in the past
and judge the newness of the present moment, based not on
the reality of the here and now but rather on associations from
the past.

Meanwhile, while we're busy in our minds comparing and
contrasting, and also creating imaginary projections into the
future about what might transpire, we've mostly lost our direct participation in the present moment, and thus separated
ourselves from true engagement in the unfolding of our lives.
We've substituted an encounter with the unique reality before us for a categorized stereotype that we then react to based
on past memories, attitudes, and assumptions.

Consider this. If you're like most people, when you pause
and look at a magnificent sunset, you're often overwhelmed by
the beauty before you. Through the powerful positive impact
of the visual experience, your thinking mind becomes temporarily quiet . . . you pop into a moment of unexpected bliss
. . . your heart and soul open up and you experience, at least
for a moment, zero sense of separation between yourself and
the world around you. You have a momentary epiphany in
which you transcend your ego boundaries and merge with
the universe of which you are an integral part.

But then what happens? Your thinking mind cuts into gear
again, your inner voice starts doing its predictable commentary on the beauty of the sunset – and suddenly the bubble
of mystic oneness and bliss is popped. You're back inside your
own ego skin once again, "thinking about" the sunset rather
than experiencing it directly beyond the bounds of cognitive
comment.

Notice clearly here that even a positive judgment – "Oh,

what a beautiful sunset that is!" – pops the experiential bubble, often just as quickly as a negative judgment does. As soon as you shift into analytical gear and engage your awareness in thinking about what kind of an experience you're having, you're no longer having that experience – you're thinking about an ephemeral encounter that has now slipped off into a memory to be rationally compared with other memories.

Let me say this again: The cognitive process of chronic judging requires that we evaluate each experience we have, in comparison with similar experiences we've had in the past – and this memory-evaluation process removes us from the experiential here and now. We lose the present moment whenever we shift into reflections about the past. To understand this primary psychological fact is to gain great insight into how our chronically judging minds continually distance us from the experience of the present moment.

The Power of Acceptance

When we're busy judging, we're definitely not accepting things just as they are. Instead our mind is creating inner dissonance by its insistence on evaluating if something should be different than it is right here, right now. This process separates us from whatever it is that we're judging.

As long as we're caught up thinking, "I don't entirely like this," or "Maybe it's not to my advantage to be spending time today with Harriet," or "This situation should be different than it is," or "Jeffrey shouldn't have done that," we can't relax and enjoy the present moment – because we've just judged the situation in such a way that separates us from it. But as soon as we say, "I accept this just as it is," or even more important, "I accept myself just the way I am," we open our hearts and embrace the world and ourselves. As we saw with Nicole, open-hearted acceptance without question is surely the path to love and enlightenment.

But still the logical mind reacts with the obvious and crucial questions: If we accept the world just as it is, how will things ever get any better? And if we accept ourselves just as we are, with all our foibles, don't we lose all impetus to work through all our old programming? Don't we condemn ourselves to mediocrity and zero change through totally accepting?

Again, good questions. To find the answers, let's take a close look at what actually happens when we stop judging and shift into full acceptance of the present moment as perfect, just as it is. This is, as we saw, exactly what Nicole did with Michael – she quieted her mind and opened her heart.

Notice carefully here that as soon as we accept our present reality without judgment, and let our love flow unconditionally into the situation, in effect we surrender all the attitudes that keep us distant and detached from the situation and thus become more lovingly involved with that situation. We become active participants, rather than judgmental observers. And by entering into such intimate participation in the unfolding present moments, our own loving presence, released from its judgmental inhibitions, begins to very actively influence the situation – so that, in fact, natural positive change is encouraged through our very presence.

By having our minds free to regularly tap our deeper spiritual wisdom and guidance regarding the situation, we will know directly from our intuitive depths when and how to act. Through the very act of accepting the world just as it is, we become a powerful agent of positive change in the world! This phenomenon – total acceptance generating positive change – definitely represents a seeming logical paradox that deserves universal exploration and application. Let's look again at the logic very carefully, because it is brought to light all too infrequently.

We tend to think that if we accept something just as it is, if we offer the world unconditional love, things are going to stay just the way they are. We assume that acceptance leads to passivity. But this isn't what happens at all. Loving acceptance leads to an active engagement that spreads our love and manifests our wisdom, and thus encourages rapid evolution of a situation. And throughout, love – not fear-based judgment – will be the motivating power.

PAUSE AND EXPERIENCE

•

After reading through this paragraph, put the book aside (if you want) and close your eyes, tune into your breathing . . . and imagine that someone you know quite well comes into the room, but doesn't see you. . . . They sit down, turn on the television, or pick up a book to read. Notice what your mind does, what thoughts emerge, as you watch this person. Don't judge your own thoughts, just observe them in action . . .

Observing Your Own Self

In that last mini-exercise, I asked you to perform a seemingly simple yet actually very challenging mental operation – that of observing your own thoughts in action. Through the simple act of looking with acceptance and love at your own judgmental habits, you will discover that you can initiate spontaneous positive change with those mental habits.

However, we all know how extremely difficult it can be to

observe our own selves (thoughts, appearance, performance, lovability, intelligence, and so on) without criticizing what we see. When you learn how to more lovingly observe your own mind's behavior (as we will discuss more deeply in Chapter 4), you'll naturally begin to effect positive change in your mental habits – without ever having to judge your thoughts as bad or wrong or faulty in order to change and quiet them.

Indeed, it seems almost impossible to improve your mind's judgmental habits toward others unless you first learn to accept yourself as perfectly okay just as you are. Self-help doesn't work without the presence of self-love. Then and only then, through the power of acceptance and love that you're shining on your own mind, does spontaneous inner healing and deep personal growth occur.

Like many of us in our civilization, I first came across this basic notion of the remarkable spontaneous healing power of love and acceptance through a childhood immersion in my family's religious tradition, where the teachings of Jesus regularly recommended "loving rather than judging" as the inner act that can change the world for the better.

But I didn't fully comprehend how this healing power of acceptance could directly evoke change until I began studying in my early twenties with yoga meditation teacher Joel Kramer. From Joel's teachings and writings (his book *The Passionate Mind* remains the classic on this topic), I came to understand that inner change is evoked not through mental manipulation or ego direction, but simply by looking without judgment and seeing clearly the habits and workings of one's own mind.

Joel presented our innate response to perceived danger in a new light. His insight, emerging from 4,000 years of yogic meditation on the workings of the mind, advances the idea that our inner mental world performs the same way as our amygdala: It is capable of responding instantly with total realization and wisdom when it perceives a danger.

Specifically, if we look clearly at our own mental habits of judging, and perceive directly the danger and damage that is being caused by a certain ingrained attitude or belief (the attitude that "I'm no good" in Nicole's case), then our organism will respond to this clear, direct inner perception by letting go of that attitude. In a word, we instantly self-correct.

Thus we can see that by creatively employing our basic "animal" response to fear in new ways, we can generate positive change within our deepest conditioned belief systems – by doing absolutely nothing at all except lovingly observing our own minds in action without engaging in judgment of any kind.

What's key, then, is learning how to enter into a state of consciousness where you can observe your thoughts, without being totally consumed in or identified with them. And this is what we're learning with the basic breath, heart, whole-body meditation that prepares your mind for such nonjudgmental observation. The instant self-correction process we seek, in moving beyond habitual judgmental thoughts, is activated only when we've shifted free of our usual past-fixated mode of thinking into the more expansive present-moment awareness of the perceptual-intuitive mind.

Joel recommended making this mental shift into nonjudgmental intuitive self-observation on a regular basis – taking time each day to observe your inner habits of mind clearly so as to perceive instantly the truth of the situation and evoke the proper inner response. The aim is to employ the self-correction power of your whole consciousness – so you respond to the mental situation at hand with your whole being, and elicit immediate self-corrective healing of detrimental mental habits you observe.

Let's say you are angry at someone at work for something they did, and you're now constantly thinking negative thoughts about them. Every time you see them or remember something about them, your mind attacks them for being stupid, or mean, or untrustworthy. If you observe yourself having these thoughts, you will see that the thoughts cause your body to tense up, your stomach to tighten, your heart to close off to this person. Now, when you encounter this person, you knock them further down rather than helping them at all.

When you see clearly that your thoughts toward this person are hurting both of you, this clear perception will be processed by the amygdala and all associated parts of the brain. Such judgmental thoughts will be labeled as dangerous mental behavior – and your mind will begin to quiet those thoughts, so as to protect your organism from the perceived danger of continuing to harbor them.

With this in mind, I encourage you to begin looking inward regularly, so that you can watch your mental habits in action and lovingly observe them. The aim is for you to begin to see more and more clearly that being habitually in judgment mode is in itself a danger to your well-being.

Every time you catch yourself judging a situation, you will catch yourself in the act of separating yourself from that situation – and thus drastically reducing your inherent ability to participate and evoke positive change. This judgmental process that separates you from the present moment is dangerous.

But note that this alertness to danger is not being generated by the deductive mind's past-conditioned judgmental function. This alertness and observation is being made in the present moment by your greater consciousness, by your higher wisdom, which includes your reason, your instincts, your loving compassion, and your intuitive, even spiritual wisdom. Your whole being sees the truth that judging separates you from living fully in love in the present moment. Therefore it's time to stop such judging. As you see this truth, you will spontaneously change.

When Jesus, the primary teacher of our Western tradition, said, "Do not judge," he was almost certainly directing attention to the grave danger inherent in the very process of judging, rather than accepting. The fact is, it doesn't matter what the particular judgment might be about – as long as you're in analytical judgment mode, you remain shut off from your spontaneous capacity to respond to the present moment fully, with your whole heart and soul.

As we will explore throughout this book, you can't love and judge at the same time. In any given situation, you have the choice between stepping back and judging, or stepping forth and participating. Obviously, to interact with the world or with your own self, without the wisdom and healing power of love being present, is ultimately to endanger your well-being. You have lost your sense of vital engagement in the unfolding of the present moment.

Therefore, it is both wise and logical to be in judgment mode as seldom as possible, and to be in love mode as often as possible. Your ego, understanding this higher logic (and, hopefully, remembering it) can now regularly help focus your attention so as to quiet judgmental thoughts and open your heart and soul.

Let's use this short exercise to gently explore your experience of watching your own thoughts flow through your mind.

PAUSE AND EXPERIENCE

•

Close your eyes, and again, think of someone you know – just whoever pops into mind. Observe what thoughts and images come to mind when you think about what upsets you about this person, what you'd like to see change or improve. . . . Now see what happens in your mind, when you temporarily just let go of all your judgments about this person and accept them just as they are, in the open-hearted spirit of love . . .

Attitude Versus Experience

When Nicole first met Michael at the party mentioned in our earlier discussion, her initial judgment of him, as she told me, was that he appeared in certain ways (the color of his eyes, the way in which he stood, the casual clothes he was wearing, his confident tone of voice) somehow similar to her last boyfriend – and therefore was someone to avoid, because that previous relationship had ended in heartbreak.

Luckily, by the time she came face-to-face with Michael, she'd already started observing her own thoughts without being totally immersed in them – and she recognized that her reaction to this new man was based mostly on past experience rather than the present moment. She was judging Michael negatively and shutting him out of her life, period.

But seeing that she was making this unfair judgment about the new man, she chose to let go of the projection (the prejudice) she was aiming at Michael and risk responding to him in the present moment. She soon discovered that, indeed, her initial assumption that he was similar to her last lover was entirely wrong. An inner learning process had occurred, which further reinforced her new habit of watching her thoughts and catching herself judging before the judgment could influence her experience.

Like Nicole, we all tend to make snap judgments – judgments that hardly register as conscious associative thought processes. Instead, because of past conditioning of our amygdala, our conscious thoughts about a situation or person become negatively colored even before we move through a realistic analysis of the situation. We almost instantly project a stereotype based on past experience onto the present moment, and begin thinking thoughts that reflect this stereotype.

This reflexive judgment is of course the very nature of prejudice. Without allowing the present moment to prove itself rightly or wrongly judged, we associate the present situation with some similar situation in the past, where we developed a dominant judgment or attitude, and react to the present situation with the same general assumption we developed in the past.

This can happen even at purely perceptual levels. One day some years ago I shaved off my beard. When my first son, then 10 years old, came home from school, he looked right at me but instead of seeing my clean-shaven face in the present moment, his mind projected my bearded face of the past onto his present-moment experience. Three times during the next half hour he looked right at my face while talking to me, without seeing that the beard was gone. Then finally the present experience overrode the past image, and he saw my face without the beard.

In each and every moment, consider to what extent you fully process the actual perceptual experience arriving in your brain, as opposed to just projecting what you expect to see onto the situation. We've all lived extremely full lives and in the process had a great many experiences that left a lasting impression on us. The older we get, unless we consciously reverse the process, the more we tend to see the present moment as a function of the past rather than as something bright and new – and often unexpected.

When we choose to stop judging a situation and simply experience it directly in the present moment, we're choosing to at least temporarily let go of our associations, and trust instead our present-moment perceptions, heartfelt emotions, and spontaneous responses. We're choosing to fully engage our lives with the uniqueness of the here and now, rather than the predictability of the that and then. We're putting aside whatever security might be found in past experience in favor of the creative newness found only in the emerging present. When we see that we have this choice, we tend to rapidly override old fear-based programmings and live more fully in the moment.

Beyond Cognition

Cognitive psychologists state in formal theory that all human beings are constantly judging the world around them through the flow of what are called "automatic thoughts." These automatic thoughts judge present situations based on past experience. For cognitive psychologists there exists a mental continuum to our attitudes and beliefs, beginning with casual assumptions and preferences, deepening into general life rules and attitudes, and solidifying into core beliefs.

During our childhood especially, we learn to associate certain types of situations and experiences with particular cognitive labels. Then, whenever we encounter a new situation that seems related to a past situation, we automatically project our prevailing attitudes, assumptions, rules, and beliefs onto that new situation. When these attitudes and assumptions are negative or unrealistic, we end up suffering.

As mentioned earlier, cognitive therapy is a very successful process that can provide some relief for such emotional and behavioral suffering – by identifying the attitudes and beliefs and resultant chronic thought-flows that are causing a behavioral problem, and by updating or changing or overriding those attitudes and beliefs with new ones that serve the individual more successfully.

A great many people have gotten relief from emotional and behavioral problems by replacing a negative or unrealistic belief or attitude with a more positive and realistic one. And I encourage you to get Judith Beck's book *Cognitive Therapy*, if you feel attracted to this approach to personal growth and healing, and explore the process further. Especially as a beginning step, if you find your fears too dominant for you to move forward with the programs in this book, a couple of months of cognitive therapy might be called for.

However, at deeper levels of healing, cognitive therapy functions through a set of core beliefs about human nature that I often find too limiting, and perhaps in need of evaluation, for the therapy system to be complete and therefore truly rewarding. Most cognitive therapists I know assume in their work that the attitude-judgment-belief structure of the human personality is the ultimate bedrock of that personality, and that all personal growth must be accomplished through correcting, changing, deconditioning, and advancing bothersome and destructive beliefs and judgments into more successful beliefs and assumptions.

The thesis of this present book and set of programs is that, yes, we do need to do our homework and identify negative beliefs that are dragging us down, and develop more realistic present-moment beliefs that serve us better. And I support cognitive therapists and all the other reality-focused therapy traditions, in their wonderful work in successfully treating symptoms.

At the same time, I hope this book will encourage the on-going professional exploration of the deeper capacity of the human organism to spontaneously self-correct through the "quiet mind" intuitive process that not only relieves symptoms but also leads to a deeper unified healing and sense of wholeness and well-being.

The Forgiveness Factor

A team of researchers led by Stanford University psychologist Carl Thorensen has recently shown that rapid emotional healing does occur when the person lets go of beliefs about blame. When we stop blaming someone, and choose to simply accept the reality of the situation, we are of course performing the basic act of forgiveness, which is the term Thorensen and team employ in their research.

They found that in weekly group therapy sessions lasting six weeks, they could generate clear positive results on several testing formats, by employing a variety of psychological techniques for helping clients do the following:

1. Shift from holding onto rigid judgmental "rules" about how other people should behave, to holding less judgmental "preferences" for how others might behave.

2. Explore and develop the belief or understanding that no adult can or should control the behavior of another person.

3. Reevaluate the hurtful incident from several different perspectives, including that of a neutral viewpoint.
4. Shift consciously away from the act of blaming toward full acceptance of what has happened to them.

The 259 adults who took part in this study showed that, after learning how to forgive, rather than blame, they were less attached to bad feelings related to a hurtful incident and also more likely to forgive in the future, compared with their control group. These positive effects were shown to continue in a six-month follow-up study. Those who learned how to let go of blame and accept reality without judgment also experienced a detectable reduction in stress, anger, and psychosomatic symptoms, in comparison with the control group.

Forgiveness is often thought of as a somewhat mystic religious process, and indeed, many religions focus strongly on the act of forgiving as part of the spiritual path. However, we can also understand and apply the power of forgiveness clearly within the psychological framework of this book by realizing that blame is based not on what someone else does or does not do in relation to us, but on what we choose to believe has happened to us as a result of what that person has done.

In other words, forgiveness is simply the cognitive act of letting go of a judgmental belief that is not serving us. When we see that holding onto the belief that someone has "hurt" us is in itself what is hurting us, we tend to let go of the hurtful belief. When we look to see the reality of the situation rather than staying stuck in our conditioned reaction to it, we in essence shift our focus of attention from the world of belief to the world of experience and let reality clarify the truth of the situation. In the process, we quiet the cognitive judgmental function of the mind and shift into more heart-

centered, compassionate, intuitive realms. We experience the
letting go of judgment, and in this act, experience the process
of forgiveness.

Let's now look with a keen eye directly at the difference between believing and experiencing.

Believing Versus Knowing

Let me share with you my own initiation into a new understanding of the difference between dealing with the world
mostly from the perspective of a belief system versus the perspective of direct experience. Back during Vietnam War when
I was just getting out of college, I chose to study for the min-
istry rather than go into the army. Ministers were draft-deferred
and it seemed a quite rational choice to make, having always
been intrigued by spiritual realms as a child, and having never
had any interest in war at all, certainly one I didn't feel was
justified.

Unexpectedly, at the seminary I found a war of another
type raging – an academic and religious war that threatened
seriously to shake the very foundations of the Christian church.
This war was being fought over the value and intrinsic nature
of the core beliefs that underlie the Judeo-Christian tradition.
A group of theologians at my seminary and elsewhere throughout the country, most of them with strong psychological as
well as theological backgrounds, were hotly challenging the
very notion of "believing" as a foundation for spiritual practice. They had carefully studied the psychological nature and
process of believing and established that believing meant "hop-
ing and accepting that something is true, without ever having
any direct experience that it is true." They pointed out the
dramatic difference between believing that there is a God,
and knowing that there is a God.

Their thesis was quite simple: Spirituality was at heart an experiential present-moment intuitive process based on direct encounter with the divine, not a cognitive process based on more and more advanced belief development.

What had the establishment up in arms was the theologians' suggestion that Christians actively let go of just believing in the precepts of the Christian Church – because that act of believing meant being satisfied with secondhand information and trusting a conceptual model, a theological idea of spiritual life, rather than trusting the direct encounter with the Spirit itself.

By the time I arrived at my (admittedly quite radical) seminary, these theologians had posited that people who "only believe in God" by definition do not have a direct experiential relationship with the divine, and that people who have this experiential relationship with God don't need beliefs at all. They know the truth, they are in communion with the Spirit in the present moment – and this direct knowing is the reality of spiritual life, not beliefs based on words and theological constructs.

Although I didn't fully support the theologians' either-or argument (for me there's nothing wrong with developing religious beliefs, as long as we also regularly tune into direct spiritual experience), I admit I was deeply struck by this general line of logic, especially where it ran parallel to other studies I was doing at the time concerning the psychology of the Buddhist and Hindu meditation experience. Meditation in whatever religion, we were discovering, was upon close analysis almost always a variation on a primal psychological process – where human beings point their mind's attention toward a present-moment encounter with the universal spiritual reality that exists beyond all words and concepts, at the center of each of our experiential reality.

We did find, in related psychological research studying the spiritual experiences of the members of several meditation communities, that most people who meditate regularly tend to consider their daily direct encounter with the divine to be vastly more important than any particular religious beliefs and rituals associated with their meditation practice.

In stark contrast, I was rather dismayed to discover that my family tradition of Presbyterian Protestantism had absolutely zero to say about meditation. There was no contemplative tradition in the Presbyterian church – no heritage or training programs for quieting the mind and communing directly with God. Instead, the Presbyterian tradition taught us to regularly "think about" God, to "talk to" God, to "believe in" God, with a heavy focus on reading the Bible – which usually proved to be yet another way to fill the mind with multitudinous religious ideas, rather than direct spiritual encounter.

But wherever I looked, there were no practical guidelines or encouragement for quieting the mind and experiencing God directly, beyond the intellect. Of course, a great many people in the Protestant tradition did (and do) have occasional spontaneous spiritual encounters with the divine. And many ministers do their best to include quiet moments in prayer, for instance, for spiritual contemplation. But in general, the study of theology proved to be just that – a study of the logic of God rather than the seeking of experience of the reality of God, even though God, by definition, is vastly more than human logic can ever grasp.

The radical theologians at my seminary were thus challenging a major Christian belief in claiming that rather than thinking logically about God, they chose to commune with God beyond the constructs of the thinking mind. They furthermore insisted that it seemed a requirement of the spiritual path that we learn to regularly quiet the thinking mind, let go all our beliefs, so as to encounter the reality and presence of God directly, even if the direct encounter fell outside the bounds of the Christian belief system. In a word, they were setting the individual free from the prevailing beliefs of the culture.

These theologians were able to turn to the Bible itself for their source dictum: Be still, and know that I am God. . . . Know the truth, and the truth will set you free. . . . Consider the lilies, and how they grow. . . . Judge not. . . . Fear not. . . . The kingdom of heaven is within.

If I'm to be honest, much of this book and of the quiet-mind guided programs had their rough origins in my participation in the holy war that was fought while I was at seminary. Step-by-step, I came to realize that, at least in my own life, I either believe that something is true, or know that something is true. I either run on secondhand knowledge and hopes and imaginations, or I run on direct encounter with the truth. And once I saw that I had the choice, there was really no choice. After all, who wants just an idea, no matter how good – when they can have the experience behind the idea.

This belief-versus-experience issue is also currently found in cognitive therapy debates regarding whether it's enough help to a client to replace one belief with another. Many therapists realize that, for a full recovery from the debilitation of limiting or self-damaging beliefs, we need to learn how to look within, beyond all our concepts and beliefs, and discover the root experiential truth of who we are – so that we know directly and don't have to trust beliefs for our ultimate security.

Many psychologists and therapists already understand this basic human need full well, and employ intuitive-shifting and meditative dimensions in their work. In the process of

helping a client to see reality more clearly and to let go of unrealistic assumptions and apprehensions, more and more therapists are turning to integrative techniques for helping the
client look inward and encounter reality beyond all words.
This is an extremely important evolution of our general therapy tradition. Be still – and know!

Whose Business Is It?

As you probably know from watching your own stream of
consciousness, a great many of your more unpleasant thoughts
tend to be caught up in judgments about situations that are
not directly your responsibility. Almost all of us have the tendency to stick our noses overmuch in other people's business.
We gossip about our neighbors and associates; we worry about
other people's problems; we get upset at things other people
do; we question decisions other people make.

In sum, we create a great deal of internal emotional upset
that does us (and usually others too) no good at all. We create suffering where there is no need, by not respecting the difference between what is our business, what is other people's
business, and what is generally beyond our control.

Below is a guideline that will facilitate the quieting of perhaps half to two-thirds of all the upsetting thoughts that your
mind habitually generates. This guideline delineates formally
what you'll discover on your own: that there are three types of
judgments you can make in life.

1. You can make judgments about your own life.
2. You can make judgments about other people and their lives.
3. You can make judgments about societal and religious
   situations and issues.

Usually this is expressed as discriminating between "my business," "your business," and "God's business." In my therapy work, one of the major steps clients make is when they begin to realize the difference between focusing their mind's attention on their own business, as opposed to having their noses in other people's business. One of the truly liberating realizations is that it's not our job in life to assume responsibility for other people and their lives. Unless those judgments influence our own lives, it's usually not our role to judge the decisions other people make, nor to apply our own "shoulds" and "should nots" to the affairs of other people. We have no inherent right to judge the actions or beliefs of other people – they have the freedom to do whatever they choose to do with their lives, within normal ethical boundaries.

But still most of us find our minds full of judgmental chatter about other people. "Harriet shouldn't have split up with Fred," or "I think it was wrong for Timmy to leave a good job and join that weird music group," or "Why did Ronaldo buy that dumb pickup truck when he can't even fit his family into it?" or "If I was Lucien, I'd definitely tell Ignacio a thing or two!"

There's nothing more bothersome and upsetting than having someone judging our own decisions and actions in life. We hate it when other people judge us, as if it's their business to evaluate our personal world. So logically, for our own part, we'd better stop judging them. It accomplishes no good, it uses up priceless energy and time, and it often leaves us feeling worse than if we hadn't had the thought in the first place. Except for such situations as making community-participation and voting decisions, and standing up for what we feel is right politically and economically, it's time to mostly let that entire category of "being in other people's business" go, so that we have more free time to enjoy the present moment with our emotions calm, our senses sharp, and our spirit bright.

And so it is with larger societal and planetary happenings, many of which were traditionally called "acts of God." Most of us spend a lot of our mental time ruminating about the war in the Middle East or the famine in Africa or the hurricane that hit the Florida coast or the fall of the stock market or the slave trade in Asia.

If we're going to actively get engaged in doing something about these acts of God or politicians or sunspots or world crises, fine. Otherwise, except again for standing up for what we feel is right politically and economically, we're wasting precious time condemning this and questioning that and in general holding our focus of attention in business that we're not directly engaged in. When a hurricane hits far away where we can do nothing to help, we don't have to engage our minds in judging the phenomenon. We do much better to accept what happens elsewhere in the world, without making it our business to ruminate about it.

PAUSE AND EXPERIENCE

•

Pause after reading this paragraph, close your eyes, tune into your breathing . . . and let yourself think of a person or situation you've been angry at or worrying about recently. Observe the way in which you tend to assume responsibility for another person's business. And then see how you feel when you stop intruding into their personal world, and say to yourself, "What they do is none of my business."

Don't Fight Reality

Let's go a step further into the dynamics of accepting rather than judging, and how this step is essential for attaining peace of mind. As you regularly look inward at your own thought-flows in the next days and weeks, you'll almost certainly come to the realization that most of your internal suffering and confusion comes about through one basic assumption of your mind – that things should be different than they are.

For instance, perhaps someone does something to you that you don't like. Instead of accepting the reality of what has happened, adjusting to what happened, and then letting go of the incident, in your mind you'll find you often continue to resist, to condemn, to judge the person and the deed as wrong and unacceptable – you refuse to accept the reality of the past, through continuing to judge it as wrong.

Here's the question: Does this chronic mental judgment and projection of blame ever benefit you, or is fixating on negative things from the past a primary cognitive habit that needs to be observed as dangerous to your well-being, and gently but definitely put aside?

In Buddhism it's said that our suffering is a direct expression of our distance from the truth. When we fully accept the reality of the past and the present moment, emotional suffering is reduced to a minimum. To the extent that we fight reality by complaining, blaming, or refusing in our own minds to accept what has happened, we suffer. Why? Because we deny what is true, and generate all sorts of negative emotions in the process.

Logically, if we want to reduce our own inner suffering, and maximize enjoyment and peace in the present moment, we do

best by accepting reality just as we find it, rather than resisting
it just because it doesn't fit one of our beliefs or assumptions
about how things should be. Certainly we continue to work
toward our goals, and run our lives so as not to repeat events
that bother us. But we don't stay stuck in denial patterns.

In general, whenever you find yourself thinking a thought
that includes the judgmental word "should," just stop right
there and take a close look at that thought. You'll find that
it's a judgment against the reality of the moment. Someone
has done something that violates how you think things should
be, and so you react, you resist, you judge and blame and fight
against the reality. The result is usually emotional trauma, and
a loss of heartfelt engagement with that person.

Whenever you catch yourself having such a "that's wrong,
they should have . . ." thought-flow, you have the choice to
continue with a line of thought that will do no good in the
world – or to immediately stop the judgment and accept the
reality before you.

The great payoff for this approach to life is that as soon as
you consciously accept the truth of the moment, your heart
can open and your intuitive mind can come into play. You
can now participate in that reality as it is – and indeed, through
your open participation, influence the next unfolding moment – so that in fact, through your acceptance of reality, reality evolves in directions that are more harmonious and
fulfilling.

Bottom line: By denying the truth with judgmental thoughts,
you shut yourself off from participation in life. By accepting
reality just as it is, you become a transformative agent in that
reality. Reality just is. You can't change the present moment.
But reality is constantly evolving, and you can participate in
that evolution.

Angry Thoughts

Another primary mental habit that pollutes our minds on a regular basis centers around fixating on particular thoughts that make us feel angry at someone or some situation. Like all our emotions, anger doesn't emerge out of a void. We get angry mostly because of judgments we make (thoughts) that place blame and guilt on other people for doing things we don't think they should have.

A great many of us tend regularly to go around smoldering with thoughts about how someone did something wrong to us or our loved ones and hurt us – and how they therefore deserve to be somehow punished in return. We discussed briefly the process of forgiveness that can break us free from being stuck in anger mode. Let's look another step deeper into this process.

The key question that continually arises when we feel angry with someone for doing something that we perceive as having hurt us in some way, is this: Is it true that they really did something they shouldn't have done? And ultimately, are they really responsible for our hurt feelings? But bluntly, do we have any right to project our beliefs of right and wrong into their lives and throw blame upon their heads? Furthermore, do we gain anything in this particular situation by fighting against the reality of what has happened, and thus making ourselves feel angry or emotionally hurt by another person's actions or inactions?

Let's review the basic psychological fact underlying such questions: Unless anger is provoked by a direct present-moment action on the part of the other person (a punch in the nose, for example), anger is almost always a response to thoughts we're running through our minds, in which we're judging a person (or situation) as having unfairly caused us damage or upset in the past, or for planning to cause us damage in the future.

In either case, even though it's our own thoughts that are provoking our negative emotions, we blame the other person for causing us to be emotionally hurt or upset.

Now, consider the reality of the impact of anger upon our system. Unless we need to charge our bodies with aggressive power and then act physically to fight or run away, the charge of anger in our bodies is never going to serve us. It's vital to see this – and then to accept the resulting logic: Thinking thoughts that make us feel angry at someone or some situation is almost always detrimental to our health and well-being. Therefore, thoughts that place blame and guilt are counterproductive in our lives. So, understanding this fact, how can we act to quiet thoughts full of anger, blame, and guilt projection?

Most angry thoughts and feelings can be defused quite readily once we learn to question whether the underlying assumption or belief that provoked our anger is valid, and therefore to our advantage to fixate upon. By identifying and challenging the belief that underlies our guilt reaction, we can directly deactivate the entire anger-blame syndrome. This is the shortest route to forgiving and moving on.

The De-beliefing Process

I first learned the basic "de-beliefing" process over thirty years ago from the founder of the Radix Institute, master therapist Charles Kelley, and have used it ever since to great advantage. Recently a contemporary spiritual teacher named Byron Katie (you might very much enjoy her new book *Loving What Is*) has developed a highly compressed and extremely effective format for evaluating if a belief is actually true or helpful –

and letting go of the belief if it is chronically generating anger or hurtful feelings. Many therapists and spiritual consultants are now using Katie's short-format de-beliefing structure in their work to great advantage, since she's cut to the bone of the process. I'll outline the primary process here and then we'll explore it in this chapter's guided session.

There are five steps to the basic de-beliefing process. I've modified them a bit here and there, to fit this particular written and experiential audio guidance application. You'll discover that whenever you find yourself thinking angry, anxious, or upsetting thoughts toward a person or situation, you can apply these five steps to help you identify and break free of the thoughts and beliefs that are holding you in the state of anger, and thus experience forgiving and emotional release:

DE-BELIEFING STEP 1: First of all, state clearly who you're angry at and why. Express the underlying thoughts that are generating the anger. For example, "I'm angry at Philip because what he said last night hurt my feelings." Ideally write your statement down.

For instance, when Nicole first came to me for therapy work, she was chronically angry at her old lover, Jack, because she thought he'd been heartlessly unkind to her when he left her for another lover. For months, she'd been feeling wounded deep down and couldn't stop blaming Jack for her inner emotional anguish. For this exercise, she said: "I'm angry at Jack because he should have been more loving toward me, rather than ruthlessly hurting my feelings."

DE-BELIEFING STEP 2: The second step is to honestly question whether the statement, and the beliefs behind the statement, are true. Why "should" another person behave the way we want them to? And why "should" they be held responsible for our feelings, if we're the ones thinking the thoughts that make us feel bad?

In our example with Nicole, for instance, was it true that Jack should have been more loving toward her? After all, why should he behave any differently than he did? Why did Nicole think she had the right to judge his behavior? And had he really been the one who hurt Nicole's feelings, or had her own thoughts actually generated her feelings of being betrayed and treated wrong? Jack did what he felt moved to do, operating from his own codes of action. Nicole came to realize that she was expecting him to live by her codes. She was very much "in his business" and judging him on her standards, when objectively, Jack had the right to live his life the way he chose. Furthermore, Jack didn't inflict emotional pain on Nicole, it was her own thoughts about being deserted and abandoned and treated wrong – her reactions to his behavior based on her own beliefs – that generated the hurt feelings. When she came to see that she was blaming him for how she managed her thoughts and emotions, she let go of the blaming.

DE-BELIEFING STEP 3: The third step in this process is to ask, "How might I be benefiting, from believing that my reaction is valid?"

In our example, with Nicole believing that Jack should have been nicer to her and not hurt her feelings, was she enjoying the anger somehow? Was it giving her a reason to behave with aggression toward Jack, or perhaps allowing her to wallow in "poor me" feelings? Was her anger blocking some deeper thought about not being adequate to sustain a love relationship? What's the positive payoff (there almost always is one) to holding onto a belief that someone has done something wrong toward us, and therefore hurt us?

DE-BELIEFING STEP 4: The fourth step in this process is to ask, "How is my life being upset or even damaged by holding onto the belief that someone has wronged me?"

When we got to this step, Nicole immediately burst forth with an entire list of how the chronic anger she held inside her against Jack was undermining her life. She was spending much of her time with her mind full of hostile thoughts; she was fantasizing all sorts of upsetting confrontations; she often found herself shaky with anger, her mind confused, her emotions a wreck. She wasn't eating right; she wasn't exercising; she wasn't nurturing other friendships – she was consumed by her feelings and thoughts of having been wronged. In a word, she was allowing her own angry thoughts to pollute her entire life.

DE-BELIEFING STEP 5: The fifth step, the primary provoker of rapid insight and "letting go," involves asking the question, "How would my life change if I let go of the belief that this person has wronged me?"

In our example, how would Nicole's feelings change, if she stopped thinking that Jack had wronged her with his actions? Would she feel better or worse if her belief changed and she stopped thinking that she'd been wronged, and that other people were responsible for her own inner feelings? In actuality she felt immediately better when she saw she didn't have to torment herself any longer by blaming another person for her feelings. Assuming responsibility for her own thoughts and feelings was a major breakthrough for her, an inner liberation from unnecessary torment. When she saw how well the process worked with Jack, she devotedly began applying the technique to any and all people in her life toward whom she felt negative emotions.

•

That's the de-beliefing process in a nutshell. I encourage you now to return to the first step of the process, write down a statement concerning someone you feel hurt you or did you wrong, or for some reason has you feeling angry toward them, and move through the steps honestly. Find out the truth about the negative emotional charge you're carrying, and, hopefully, resolve that negative feeling rapidly.

Nothing Good nor Bad

When we judge another person or situation, we're saying that we have the power and wisdom to know what is good and what is bad. Do we, in truth, have this power? William Shakespeare hit the proverbial nail on the head when he had one of his characters say in a play, "There's nothing good nor bad, but thinking makes it so."

All religions, cultures, and social groups try to control the behavior of their members by creating lists of rules of what is accepted and what is not accepted. Often these rules are given the weight of a religious dictum, and the moral play is acted out generation after generation.

I have no argument with general rules of behavior that indicate the accumulated wisdom of a civilization. However, it's important to notice when wise suggestions get turned into a right-or-wrong format, as they all too often do. The very notion of good and bad, of right and wrong, is, upon careful analysis, not a product of the higher intuitive function of the mind. Many religious dictums might have been built upon higher rational logic, but turning a wise observation into right and wrong locks the wisdom into a fear-based judgment in a dualistic cognitive system.

Unfortunately from the time we are very young, most of us are subjected to a barrage of verbal statements and beliefs which we accept, not on the basis of experience or even rational wisdom, but simply because we've been programmed to believe they're true – and we're afraid of what might happen to us if we even question them.

There's nothing inherently right or wrong, of course, with living our lives based on rules we've inherited from our forebears. However, as we're exploring in this book, we do have mental facilities that enable us to transcend rules and beliefs that dictate with verbal cues how we "should" think and act in life. Rather than using core beliefs and unquestioned fear-based rules to control and inhibit our behavior, we can use our higher intuitive and spiritual sensibilities to guide us through life – free from the fear of right or wrong.

The key issue here is whether you trust your higher mental functions (the integrative intuitive perception of a quiet peaceful mind) to guide you so that you can set yourself free in the present moment, to act spontaneously as your heart and soul so move you. Otherwise, you're going to continue running your life based on what you should or should not do – based on assumed beliefs and regulations that may or may not reflect the best choice in the present moment, which has never existed before, and which ideally should be free to evolve however the present moment – not the past – dictates.

Let's pause again, to let you reflect upon your own feelings about what we've been discussing. After reading the next paragraph, put the book aside for a moment. Close your eyes if you want to.

Negative Core Beliefs

There's a final step we need to take, in fully exploring the process of judgment in our lives. A great many of us go around constantly blaming other people for all our problems. An equal number go around blaming themselves for being no good, for being guilty, for being wrong . . . for being somehow unacceptable.

At the heart of this basic blaming routine are two core beliefs that seem to underlie almost all the problems that people bring to the therapist's couch: the belief and feeling of being helpless; and the belief and feeling of being unlovable or unworthy.

These core beliefs are usually developed early in life and often become submerged and even inactive unless extreme life situations are confronted. But such primal cognitive substrata will continue to subtly influence the general quality and content of the thoughts and resultant emotions a person manifests in life, until openly confronted and reconsidered.

For instance, when someone is blaming others for their problems, they're almost always actually feeling helpless and weak deep down, unable to fight for their own rights. They often have the habit of holding themselves chronically caught up in anger to help bolster their underlying sense of being weak and helpless. Being helpless makes us feel frightened, and anger is a way of trying to overcome the feeling of being helpless.

In like manner, a great many people suffer tremendously and chronically from depression and guilt, and furthermore sabotage opportunities for establishing loving relationships, because early in life they developed a core belief that they're somehow hopelessly unlovable. Feeling basically unworthy of being loved leads to an entire ugly host of negative emotions, chronically being provoked by mostly subliminal thoughts running through the mind. When these thoughts are brought to the surface, they're usually spoken in a young child's sobbing voice. "Nobody loves me." "I'm not good enough." "It's all hopeless; I'm no good."

In most cases, these two core negative beliefs (assuming one is deep-down helpless and unlovable) are, as I mentioned, usually not conscious. Instead, they quietly give rise to secondary beliefs and assumptions that in turn generate recurrent thoughts such as "I don't think I'm good enough to do that," or "I'll probably fail with that anyway, so why try?" or "That's too dangerous, I'd better not do that," or "Why is life so cruel?"

As we're learning, one of the truly powerful techniques that we can apply to help heal unrealistic negative core beliefs is the process of listening without judgment to our own recurring self-debasing thoughts – and step-by-step, begin to identify the core beliefs that underlie our secondary attitudes and assumptions about ourselves and life. Then we apply the basic de-beliefing process to whatever belief we find.

For instance, you might find yourself wanting to approach someone and ask for a date – but instantly, you're hit with the thought and the feeling, "No, it's hopeless, she'll just reject me." As soon as you identify such a thought, write it down, and run it through the de-beliefing process. Let me walk you through it again, applied not to anger but to any belief:

1. State your underlying assumption: For instance, you're not worthy of someone's attention because you're basically unlovable.

2. Rationally consider if the statement is true, based on who you are now as an adult: Are you truly so totally unlovable, or is that just some old attitude about yourself that needs reconsideration?

3. Consider what you gain from holding onto the belief that you're basically not lovable. Does this attitude serve you well? Does it enable you to attain what you want in life?

4. Reflect upon whether your life is being upset or damaged by holding onto the belief that you are basically unlovable. Does this attitude make you feel depressed or lonely?

5. Now consider how your life would change if you let go of the assumption that you're not lovable and began to nurture a self-image in which you not only love yourself, but are quite worthy of other people's love.

This de-beliefing process can be augmented considerably if you decide to keep a thought diary in which you regularly pause to write down the thoughts that have just been running through your mind. Get it down on paper. Find out what your unconscious mind is chronically fixating upon. Write down all the negative thoughts, judgments, assumptions, and beliefs that come flowing through your mind. Begin to catch those secondary and core beliefs that undermine your positive experience of life by chronically pushing negative thoughts through your mind. Also of course, write down the positive enjoyable thoughts that tend to flow through your mind.

In a word, get to know yourself – and in the process of getting to know yourself, you'll begin to have realizations that will transform your beliefs for the better. We saw earlier how the simple act of observing your thoughts will very often spontaneously heal and transform them. Your job is to shine the bright light of your attention directly on the source of your thoughts and see what you find there. In this act, you'll discover which of your core beliefs are not serving you well, and in that very seeing, you'll naturally begin to let go of such beliefs.

Right here, remember, you don't have to replace old beliefs with new beliefs. In the place of those old negative beliefs, rather than trying to come up with a positive cognitive attitude toward yourself, you have the freedom of living your life more and more free of the domination of beliefs in general, by spending more time in spontaneous interaction with the world in the present moment.

Here's the trick: When you are asked who you are, or when you ask yourself that question, instead of looking to your memory banks, instead of looking to your beliefs, look instead directly to the heart of your feeling of being alive right now, in this present moment. You are, after all, a human being, not than a "human been." Who you are is to be found in how you spontaneously and with your whole being respond to the newness of the present moment. That's you! And that's not a judgment, that's an experience.

It's now time to approach our second major guided session, which will build on the basic breathing, heart, whole-body meditation you learned in the first chapter and then take you through the basic process you learned in this second chapter for evaluating your beliefs and judgmental habits, and moving beyond them. In the process we'll be focusing plenty of healing love in the direction of your own core of being, so that you nurture your relationship of total acceptance and love toward yourself. As with all the sessions of this basic program, you'll want to do this session fairly regularly, to advance rapidly into higher states of being.

GUIDED SESSION 2:
QUIETING YOUR JUDGMENTS
•

For this session, go ahead and make yourself comfortable either sitting up or lying down. Notice what you're mind is busy with right now.

When you're ready, turn your attention away from thoughts, toward your perceptual world. Feel the sensation of the air rushing in and out of your nose or mouth as you breathe . . . expand your awareness to also include the movements in your chest and belly as you breathe . . . expand your awareness to also include your heart, beating right in the middle of your breathing experience. . . . Be aware of your whole body, here in this present moment . . .

Notice if you're carrying any angry or depressed or judgmental charges in your mind and body today toward someone. . . . Look inside, and see if there's anyone or any situation in your life that you're feeling irritated about, or angry with, or depressed about . . .

Go ahead and complete the following sentence with

whatever name comes to mind: "I'm angry at (or upset by) _____ because they _____."

Are you sure that this statement is true? How do you know that they did something to you that they shouldn't have?

Are you somehow enjoying or benefiting from believing that this person did something they shouldn't have done to you, or failed to do something they should have done? What's the positive payoff, if any, for continuing to feel angry or upset?

On the other hand, are you suffering – is your life being pulled down – by continuing to think angry or resentful thoughts about this person and what you blame them for doing?

What would happen – how would your life change – if you chose to stop fighting reality, and accept entirely what this person has done, or failed to do, to you? If you just forgave and forgot and let go of the belief of being wronged, how would you feel right now?

Stay aware of your breathing . . . consider all your angry and upset feelings in general . . . and ask yourself, does getting angry and upset actually help you, or hinder you, in creating the life you want?

How would your life change if you decided to let go of the belief that other people are regularly doing bad and hurtful things to you? What if you assumed full responsibility for your own feelings?

Imagine that you're in a fairly large comfortable living room, sitting on the sofa . . . feeling good inside your own body, relaxed and at peace . . . and someone who often makes you feel angry or upset walks into the room. Stay aware of your breathing, don't react to the presence of this person . . . instead, imagine walking over to this person and, no matter how bothersome they act or talk, don't react with anger. See what happens when you feel no fear and refuse to react with anger . . . keep your heart open and your feelings calm and accepting . . .

Now imagine this person leaving the room. You're alone again, sitting on the sofa, watching your breathing and enjoying the present moment . . . you look over to the door, and see someone enter . . . imagine seeing your own self walking through the door . . .

When you meet this very familiar person's eyes, what emotion do you find there? How does this person usually feel? What is your opinion of this person – are you full of judgments toward this person, or do you accept this person just as he is, she is? Do you feel love in your heart for this person?

Now you can let go of that imagination, tune into your breathing . . . your feeling in your heart for your own self. . . . Notice what emotions are stimulated inside you, when you say or think, "I accept myself just as I am." Allow your heart to open . . .

Now, imagine that someone who is your friend, or who you'd like to become friends with, comes walking into the room. See if you can accept them with an open heart, not judging them . . . stay aware of your breathing, your whole-body presence . . . walk over to them with your mind quiet . . . perhaps give them a hug . . . enjoy the pure feeling of unconditional love . . .

Okay, you can let go of that imagination . . . just experience your breaths coming and going without making any effort to breathe . . . and as the music plays, be open to new insights, and new experience.

For streamed-audio guidance through this experience, go to www.johnselby.com.

chapter 3

breaking free from worries

We now come to the real payoff to this discussion, the resolution of the psychological murder mystery that's been lurking here. Who really is busy being the killjoy in our lives? Who's responsible for continually killing off so many of our opportunities to relax into the here and now, and have good heartfelt fun?

We've seen how the mental process of chronic judgment separates us from full participation in the present moment – as long as we're in judgment mode, we can't also be in pleasure mode. But if this is true, and it's also true that human beings prefer pleasure to pain, then why do we continually keep on judging everything that's happening around us, rather than just letting judgment go so we can spontaneously participate in the emotional depth and fun of life?

The answer requires the consideration of just one little four-letter word, but those four letters tend to dominate a considerable amount of our lives, and mostly for the worse. The word is FEAR – and more specifically, one particular aspect of fear called anxiety, where the thinking mind fixates on possible problems and provokes anxiety with worrisome thoughts, regularly disturbing our peace of mind.

In this chapter we're going to look deeper into our human fear response, identify the nature of our chronic worrying habits – and then learn the basic techniques for quieting the worried flow of upsetting thoughts that tend to noisily pollute otherwise beautiful and peaceful days.

I would like to state again that this book compresses a great deal of information and pragmatic treatment suggestions between two covers. For most of you, reading these pages and working over time with the online guided audio programs will be adequate help for you to make steady progress in letting go of troublesome thoughts that are upsetting your life. However, severe anxiety conditions and panic disorders can require the extra help of an in-person therapy relationship, and I encourage you to seek out professional help if you need hands-on help beyond these written and online programs.

Let's take a recent example from my therapy work to explore how anxious thoughts tend to keep people uptight, apprehensive, and shut off from positive feelings of peace and enthusiasm and spontaneous connection with the world. This example is probably more intense than your own, but by looking at extremes, we can often more easily understand how to tame milder worry habits.

Consumed by Worry

Peter and Jennie were actually considered to be among the more lucky folk of the late 1990s. Working together in their small computer software company, they'd come up with a truly brilliant high-tech concept, plugged it into the then-burgeoning e-commerce market, raised $3 million from friends, and pushed their company to its initial public offereing in less than eleven months. At that point, because of Peter's health problems, they bailed from the corporation with loads of cash – enough to live several lifetimes – and moved to Hawaii for their twentieth wedding anniversary.

I was introduced to Peter a year later through a mutual friend who was also Peter's doctor. His recurrent ulcer and digestive problems were still giving him serious trouble even though he'd retired early to paradise; his alcohol consumption remained considerable even though drinking made his health condition worse; and psychologically, even though his future seemed secure, he was overly irritated, aggressive, and all too often a nervous wreck.

I soon found that Jennie wasn't faring much better – she was worried about her husband's health and emotional condition, and an entire list of other life problems as well, leaving her plagued with bouts of anxiety and often unable to enjoy the climate and beaches of her new home.

With such situations, I usually allow people to talk themselves into their own realizations, and since he was a smart and honest person, it didn't take Peter long to begin to hear what he was saying as he described his daily life to me. I would ask a simple question such as, "Well, day in and day out, what is it that gets you upset most?" and he'd launch into a ninety-minute exposé of a life that was riddled with hostile judgments, aggressive thoughts, judgmental suspicions, and chronic worrying.

"You can't imagine," he told me during our first informal meeting out on his expansive lawn overlooking the Pacific Ocean, "just how stressful it can be, having to keep up-to-date

on all my investments. I'm continually having to hassle about
the market, about every investment I have. I sit down at my
computer or get on the phone, and almost every day I un-
earth a crisis somewhere that threatens my situation, or come
across somebody in charge that I don't really trust to handle
the situation. It's enough to drive anybody crazy, just waking
up every morning to face so much uncertainty, so many potentially disastrous money situations. It all comes down to
who can you trust – and some days, it seems like there's nobody really responsible out there in charge. I feel like I'm still
carrying the weight of running things on my back, even though
I'm supposed to be retired. How can you retire when the
money has to be managed or it'll just go right down the drain
and leave you without a penny? I've seen it happen to other
people – it could happen to me the minute I let down my
guard."

When I talked with Jennie a couple of days later, she responded to the same basic question about what worried her
with her own expression of constant inner turmoil: "I watch
Peter still undermining his health," she complained. "He won't
listen to me at all. I'm so glad you're working with him now.
I feel helpless; he worries me to death; he has everything in
life but he's still miserable. And our boy Jasper is just the same;
he's bent on ruining his life, living off in Lesotho, some tiny
country right in the middle of South Africa – imagine – and
he's working right out with the natives, trying to help them
raise better corn or some such thing. He could have his throat
slit; he could get AIDS. I go to bed at night worrying and
praying for him, but what can I do? And on top of that, I have
my own mother; she's 68 and now that Dad's gone, she's living alone at the house in New Haven with no one to take care
of her. I keep telling her she should move out here with us,

that something could happen to her and I wouldn't even know it for days. And now to make matters worse, we have new neighbors and I'm certain they're spraying their whole place with some pesticide to kill the mosquitoes – and we're down-wind from them, and I've called the health department but they haven't done anything; we're just sitting here breathing death every day. I told Peter we'd have to move, and he said he'd go over there this afternoon to talk with them – but you know he has a bad stomach; he's not supposed to do anything that gets him angry, I'm afraid he'll get into a fight and . . . "

And so on and so forth. They talked and talked about what worried them and made them angry, until finally they began to see for themselves that they were living their lives consumed by thoughts that caused them to suffer the constant agony of hostility, anxiety, and apprehension. Step-by-step I began to educate them with the same information we're discussing in this book – the basic understanding of how our own thoughts can hold us in an interior torture chamber – and fairly quickly, they began to get the point.

"But I still can't quite accept what you're saying," Peter con-fronted me at one point. "You're saying that I can just quiet my mind and let go of being tough and aggressive. But that's crazy – if I stop struggling, if I just trust things to work out, if I walk away and let things take their own course, I'd be a goner. I'd lose everything."

I'd already explained to Peter that all angry feelings, and indeed most of one's stressful problem-solving behavior, emerge from a core sense of being in danger – in other words, fear is at the heart of anger, provoking the "fight" reflex to protect from a danger. But rather than argue the point that we don't need fear to motivate our business activities, instead I sug-gested that Peter take a close look at the underlying belief he'd just expressed – that if he stopped fighting to succeed, he would lose everything and be a goner. Was this assumption actually valid?

It took Peter only a few minutes to logically think through his assumption and realize that the belief wasn't true at all. His chronic worrying and feelings of aggression weren't saving him from losing everything. In fact these emotional and mental states were directly taking away his most prized possessions – his health and peace of mind.

"So why do I continue worrying and struggling like I do if it's obviously not helping me?" he finally asked. "I'm a smart guy – are you saying that I'm running my mind in a stupid way? It's you who's talking nonsense. You're recommending a completely suicidal approach to life."

I calmly pointed Peter's attention one step deeper into his core belief, which was beginning to come to the surface – namely, that if he didn't worry about the future, he'd lose everything. It took only about twenty minutes before he was realizing that underneath all his worries about losing his fortune, underneath his habitual lack of trust in other people he was involved with, was the core fear that at any time, if he wasn't careful and constantly on the alert for danger signs, he would be taken advantage of, lose absolutely everything, have no food or home, and end up dying destitute out on the beach.

This core fear was of course entirely irrational – but there it was, an abject assumption of radical danger around every business curve, an assumption that he had harbored ever since he could remember. In fact, upon closer analysis, he realized his father had held this same fear, and probably his grandfather as well.

Through the power of calm clear reason, Peter discovered that his underlying childhood or inherited fear of losing everything and dying destitute if he didn't constantly worry and fight about business was not a valid fear. When he played out the drama in the clear light of present-moment reality, he found that he was indeed letting his life be driven by a core assumption that was not realistic. Even if all failed, he'd take care of himself. He wasn't a victim personality at all.

And his habit of allowing himself to be pushed around by an irrational, mostly subconscious fear had nothing to do with inherent intelligence. The problem wasn't being generated by lack of intelligence. It was being perpetuated by lack of observation of his own mind's inner workings.

I kept helping Peter return his focus of attention to areas of his inner functioning that, throughout his life, he had habitually ignored. The same basic process helped Jennie as well. She gained a conceptual understanding of how the mind works and how habits of worrying undermine one's life – and soon she began to realize, from carefully watching recurrent thoughts come and go, that everywhere she looked in her life, she tended to project a basic anxiety about one underlying negative theme – the possibility of someone she loves dying and leaving her alone.

She was habitually worrying herself sick imagining all sorts of deadly scenarios that might happen to various friends and family members. And her mind got so engrossed in these anxious fantasies that they generated the same anguish she would experience if the event was actually happening in real life. Instead of having to undergo the trauma of a death in the family only when it actually happened, she was forcing herself to experience the trauma over and over.

Finally we were looking right at the core fear that scared her the most – the reality of death itself, the final chapter of everyone's life. After struggling to even talk about it, she managed to tell me amidst a great many tears that when she was 7 years old, her older sister had died in a car accident, and ever since then she'd had a terrible fear of all things related to death.

Now it was time for her to finally face the fact that everyone dies – that none of us are going to get out of this alive after all, and that death is something we can face and accept, rather than fearing and becoming obsessed with. As Jennie came to accept at deep levels that she was mortal and of course would die someday, her worries began to ease up dramatically.

As I mentioned earlier, Jennie and Peter faced some fairly stiff anxiety habits. They had to devote adequate time to understanding how their minds work from the inside out, and they then had to face their dangers directly and shine the light of reason and adult perspective on their buried fears and illusions from the past. They also needed to quietly observe their attitudes and beliefs about life, and actively remember to quiet their minds whenever old mental habits of worrying rose again to the surface.

But overall, in six weeks they were able to see their primary danger (their own worrying habits and fearful core beliefs) and let go of mental habits that didn't serve them. In the process of accepting life just as it is, and also of accepting death as a natural part of life, they were able to embrace life rather than fight against it, and thus live it more fully. And in this process, they both began to experience a quieting of their minds in general, as they regularly shifted beyond thoughts, to direct enjoyment of the present moment.

Of course, like everyone, these two people remain human and will tend to slip back into old worry habits now and then. And they'll certainly still experience the usual physiological reactions of fear to present-moment dangers. They'll also continue to project into the future and imagine varying scenarios, some of them upsetting, as they consider taking a future action that might result in a dangerous enterprise.

But they now have in hand the basic mental tools needed to manage their minds so that they don't continually torment themselves through chronically entertaining irrational fears about the future. They know how to direct their minds so that most of the time, they're free from the grip of fear in their lives.

Fear Versus Anxiety

You perhaps already noted that Peter and Jennie were not suffering from reactions to real-life immediate threats to their well-being. Rather, they were engaging in a special version of the fear response in which the higher functions of the mind remember frightening incidents in the past and project these memories and imaginations into the future – thus stimulating a genuine fear reaction in the emotions and body, based not on an actual danger in the present moment but on an imagined danger in the future. In a word, anxiety.

Let's expand our understanding of the human fear response a few key steps beyond the discussions of previous chapters. Please bear with me for a few pages as I get fairly specific about the neurology of fear. Like all other animals on this planet, life for us can be dangerous if we're not heads-up. Therefore our entire nervous system is designed to detect danger, and respond to it appropriately. For better or worse, our hardwiring for dealing with danger and attack is millions of years old – designed to respond to overt physical attack, in most cases, by instantly building a massive energetic charge and releasing that charge immediately by fighting like a madman or running like hell.

But in our world today, most of our dangers in life are no longer physical. Nevertheless, our bodies respond to any perceived or imagined danger through full physiological charging. Much of the negative experience of anxiety is that we develop a high charge of hormonal and muscular readiness for physical action but never release that charge through movement. Instead, like Peter, we're left with a body on red alert because of chronic worries – and this physiological charge ends up a stressor to our system, undermining our physical health as well as our emotions.

Our basic brain design started out half a billion years ago as a small clump of nervous tissue at the end of the spinal cord of our reptilian ancestors. It has evolved into four structures piled on top of the modern human spinal cord – the brain stem, the cerebellum, the diencephalons, and the cerebral hemispheres. The brain stem, consisting of the medulla, the pons, and the midbrain, controls automatic functions of the internal organs and muscles. When I suggest you become aware of your breathing, you are turning your focus of attention to the medulla, which controls your breathing and your heartbeat as well. When the amygdala detects danger, it can signal your breathing and your heartbeat to respond instantly with readiness for intense whole-body action. You gasp for air with an inhale when you're suddenly scared, yes?

The cerebellum, just behind the brain stem at the lower back of the brain, controls voluntary movements. When I suggest that you be aware of your breathing, and allow it to calm down, you are integrating the action of the medulla with the action of the cerebellum. The cerebellum is also directly linked to your primitive fear system, which can instantly give orders to the cerebellum to move the body in such a way as to avoid pain or injury. There is also emerging evidence that the cerebellum somehow influences the flow of thoughts through the mind, shifting the content instantly away from whatever it's dwelling upon and toward survival activity.

On top of the brain stem is the diencephalon, containing the hypothalamus and the thalamus, which process all sensory information flowing into the brain and regulate the flow of hormones in the body. When the amygdala registers a danger, it instantly orders the hypothalamus to secrete the key emergency hormone corticotropin-releasing factor, which primes the entire organism for fight or flight through a cascade of hormones and neurochemicals in the body and brain. The thalamus likewise serves to orchestrate orders from the fear center, in its core role as initial processing and switching center for all sensory inputs arriving in the brain. Working with the amygdala, it instantly routes perceptual information to the rational fear system in the front of the brain for further analysis.

Surrounding the diencephalon and brain stem are the two largest structures in the brain, the cerebral hemispheres, which generate all higher mental functions, including consciousness. The wrinkled outer covering of the cerebral hemispheres is the cerebral cortex, the highest level of complexity the brain has achieved to date. And as noted before, deep within the cerebral hemispheres is the ancient limbic system – the home of the amygdala, which regulates our primitive fight-or-flight fear responses.

In the human brain, as opposed to other animals, the amygdala is deeply connected and interacts intimately with a number of other brain centers to orchestrate a danger-fear response. It's clear that researchers are far from unearthing the total picture of how the brain perceives and responds to a potential danger. With 100 billion information-processing cells to work with, and a total number of 100 trillion possible connections between neurons, the extent of extremely rapid two-way communication between the primitive fear system in the center of the brain and the rational fear center located in the prefrontal cortex staggers the imagination.

Rather than just imagining, I encourage you to experience directly and regularly the impact of the perception of potential danger upon our system. In the days to come, be more and more aware of your inner experience every time you find yourself reacting suddenly to the danger signals of the primitive fear system. Feel that sudden jolt of tension and readiness caused by some external sensory input . . . and very closely, observe from the inside out how your rational fear system comes into play as you begin analyzing and thinking about the danger the amygdala has perceived. We saw in an earlier discussion of Joel Kramer's "see and change" model that to watch your own system in action offers you the ultimate opportunity to directly evoke change in that system. Be sure to allow yourself this opportunity for direct inner growth regularly throughout each new day.

The Fear-Love Continuum

The amygdala seems to be key in generating all the primary emotions, ranging from total ecstasy to passive peace to utter terror. An emotional continuum exists from one extreme, where we feel zero fear, to the other extreme, where we anticipate instant annihilation.

Indeed, many researchers feel that fear is the primal emotion from whence all the other emotions have evolved. Each emotion can be viewed as a direct expression of the particular level of fear or not-fear being assessed by the amygdala at the time. Fear, for instance, can provoke anger inside us when we are fighting to preserve our integrity. Fear can also generate the emotion of hopelessness when we can see no escape. Fear sometimes is experienced as excitement and even exhilaration when we're anticipating a challenge or winning a battle.

In other situations, overpowering fear can generate mental confusion and disorientation. Fear is certainly the core cause of the emotion of jealousy, where we are afraid of losing someone we think we need. And fear lies at the heart of the feeling of abandonment and grief, where we're afraid we can't survive when separated permanently from someone we depend on.

What about the more positive emotions? Consider simple contentment and happiness – aren't they the result of feeling that we're not in danger and can therefore relax and enjoy life? And the experience of being in love – when someone loves us we feel relatively safe from danger and protected in the same way we felt when we were babies with our mothers. Similarly, with the rush of mastery and self-confidence, we're emotionally amped because we're performing well and therefore not afraid of failing to survive.

I consider this totally fear-based analysis of human emotions interesting for as far as it takes us, but obviously there's always a vast leap to be made from the purely materialistic, nuts-and-bolts view of human experience to the actual experience of consciousness itself. Take the phenomenon of love, for instance. We all know from inside out that it exists. Jesus went so far as to say that "God is love," which equates love with the infinite creative power and potential of the universe and beyond. But what can the scientific method tell us about love – that it is nothing more than a derivative physiological reaction emanating from the primitive fear system of the brain? And how about consciousness itself? The scientific method still hasn't discovered consciousness at all.

Experimental science, as we all know, is based solely on discernable phenomena that can be registered by machine sensitivity in the outside perceptual world, and then can be repeated over and over in various laboratories. If a machine can't detect it, and if it can't be repeated, then from the scientific point of view, it doesn't exist.

At the opposite end of the spectrum, the inner phenomena of human consciousness and heartfelt love represent a purely present-moment inner phenomenon that, by the very nature of the uniqueness of each new moment, can never be repeated. Nor can machines register the presence of anything called consciousness or love – at least not so far. We know they exist because we have direct inner experience that they exist. But in the classic realms of the scientific method, they simply... aren't.

It's important to understand the amazing depths of science, and also its serious limits, when seeking to understand who we are and how we can improve our lot through conscious action.

That said, what can science tell us about who we are, and how our fear reaction relates to our conscious experience? Michael Davis, a psychiatrist at Yale University School of Medicine, recently found that when the two amygdalae are experimentally removed from mice, the mice lose all ability to feel fear. They can be placed with a cat, for instance, and instead of panicking as they usually do, they will fearlessly play with the cat.

The same phenomenon has also been demonstrated with aggressive breeds of monkeys that instinctively react with screaming and escape behavior when confronted with human beings. When their primitive fear system is removed from their brain (an ugly idea in itself), they exhibit zero fear reaction when human beings appear. In fact, the studies report that the altered monkeys will demonstrate no category of emotional reaction at all.

This research certainly indicates a direct relationship between the functioning of the amygdala and our general emotional condition. Furthermore there seems little doubt that the primal "animal" emotions of fear and aggression are grounded in our basic biological need to avoid immediate dangers so we can survive at least a bit longer. The basic fear reaction is a remarkable biochemical system that does its best to keep us from getting hurt or killed.

The fact that this system has a tendency in our contemporary world to turn into its opposite by inducing a chronic state of anxiety and worrying doesn't mean that fear is our enemy. What it means is that we need to learn how to manage our fear responses so they don't drive us crazy or ruin our health or both.

The key to developing a successful approach to dealing with our ingrained fear reactions lies in accepting that occasional fear reactions are a natural part of life, and also knowing that whenever you're not directly in physical danger in the present moment, you don't have to feel fear (anxiety and worry) at all. Instead of letting your thoughts suck you into fear mode, you can always choose to live your life in what I call, for lack of a better term, love mode.

In our own minds, we can distinguish between a genuine threat to our well-being in the present moment, in which we definitely need to play out the fear response to our advantage, and an imagined threat to our future well-being, which we need to nip in the bud and not allow to upset us. We need to be on alert for the sudden emergence of the feeling of anxiety in our bodies, and immediately identify the thought process that generated it – and quiet that thought process.

Let's turn our attention beyond the theory of fear reduction, toward actual techniques that will allow you to quell anxious thoughts whenever they arise, so that peace of mind and emotion can be regained.

Success Without Worry

As we saw in action in Peter's case, it is the unique fate of the human species to have the ability to imagine the possibility of something terrible happening in the future, and to experience in the present moment the full emotional and physiological reaction to that imagined happening. Thus we can (and very often do) worry ourselves sick, as we inflict excruciating emotional pain on our own selves – even in the absence of any real threat at all. Peter and Jennie were doing just this with all their worries about what might happen in the future, even though their present moment and probable future were quite rosy indeed.

A great many physiological studies on stress have demonstrated without question that maintaining a chronic fearful state of mind and body (worrying, being angry or aggressive, holding a constant state of readiness to fight or escape) does not serve anyone well. Chronic stress caused by too much worrying generates mental and physical fatigue, confusion, impatience, difficulty in all aspects of communication and relating. Worrying gets us nowhere fast.

If we agree that this is true, then the question at hand is clear: How do we purposefully break beyond the grip of habitual worrying and stressful posturing? Let's look at how Peter dealt with this challenge. There are probably quite a few of you still questioning whether it's actually wise for a businessperson to actively put aside worrying and nurture a quiet mind in the workplace. After all, isn't the seemingly inherent stress of worrying about deals and personnel and performance and all the rest just a natural ingredient of the business experience?

Bottom line: Would anyone with stock in a company feel comfortable if the CEO announced publicly that he was going to just stop worrying about the success of the business, and enjoy his experience of running the company?

I for one would actually feel more than comfortable. In fact, I'd salute the CEO for having made the most astute business move of his career. Why? Because as we've seen, except for sudden bursts of physical endurance, and brief flashes of heightened mental clarity that don't last beyond a few minutes at most, fear is the number one killer of high performance and mental brilliance. It numbs the deeper heartfelt emotions that enable a CEO to establish significant business relationships and trusting alliances. A CEO who's running on anxiety is not an optimum corporate leader, as I've pointed out many many times in the business community.

Peter made a list for me one morning, of all the stressors pressing down on his back that day, all the fiscal worries he was struggling with, all the anxious personnel situations he was trying to resolve. With each of the items on the list, we went through a basic procedure that showed him clearly that worrying was not going to help him resolve the business issues to his advantage. In fact, worrying was going to undermine his effectiveness considerably.

We then explored the nature of the core fear that was chronically pushing him into anxious or aggressive feelings related to business deals. By imagining the worst scenario, and then realizing that his anticipated fear was almost always vastly overamped compared to a realistic assessment of the situation, he quickly defused the worry.

Anti-Worry Procedure

Let's dig into process now. Whenever you find yourself angry, tense, worried, or confused, at work or at home or in any other situation, and a simple reshifting of your mind's focus of attention to the present moment (as you've learned already) doesn't calm your mind, you can apply this basic process for identifying and moving beyond the ultimate fear that lurks behind each and every one of your everyday worries and concerns.

As mentioned before, most surface anxieties have their roots in either the fear of abandonment (helplessness) or the fear of being unlovable – both of which ultimately in the very old cave-folk days would lead to loss of tribal support, and eventually death. The key issue is this: Are you really totally helpless or totally unlovable – and if not, why are you continually feeling afraid that you are?

ANTI-WORRY STEP 1: State the worry that's gripping you. What is the present or future situation that you're anxious about? Take time and word this worry in one clear sentence.

ANTI-WORRY STEP 2: In your mind's imagination, explore the worst-possible scenario to the ultimate limit: What are you really afraid might happen?

ANTI-WORRY STEP 3: Now surrender and accept whatever fate may bring you in the future. Ultimately, accept your eventual death.

ANTI-WORRY STEP 4: Now, using the brightness of your reasoning mind, reflect, and consider if your present worry is realistic. Is your worst-possible scenario really what would happen to you in real life, or is it a gross exaggeration?

ANTI-WORRY STEP 5: Realize that the mental habit of worrying about a possible future event is causing you immediate suffering in the present moment, and therefore is not a healthy or loving thing to do to yourself.

ANTI-WORRY STEP 6: Move entirely beyond your worrying and shift into present-moment enjoyment where you reap the immediate benefits of the procedure. Tune into your breathing . . . your heartbeat . . . your whole-body presence here and now. . . . You're no longer being plagued by worries, and therefore you're free to be fully "here" and while in this state, to choose where next to focus your attention.

Very possibly, once you've shifted out of worry mode, you'll find that you want to now go ahead and carry forth with the business at hand – but without the anxiety and emotional stress that was earlier attached to the situation. In this new state of mind, you'll find that you perform much better intellectually, that your heart is open to whatever relating comes with the work, and that you enjoy the business at hand.

Fear of Flying

Let's take another fairly intense example of how anxiety can disturb a person's life. Jennie needed to fly to LA with Peter on a family visit, and she had developed an extreme fear of flying. Here's her story, taken from her own notes, of how she dealt successfully with this fear, even though it was a great challenge.

Jennie woke up on the morning of her trip to Los Angeles and looked out their bedroom window to where a few light fluffy clouds were rushing briskly over the blue skin of the ocean. Birds were singing and flitting from tree to tree in the garden. For a few moments, she felt immersed in the beauty of the morning, her world totally at peace.

Then the thought hit her like a mean stick. This was the morning when she and Peter were boarding a jet for Los Angeles to visit his parents – yikes! She felt her breathing instantly tense, her heart start racing, her consciousness contract away from bliss of the present moment as it fixated upon the danger she faced. She'd always had a fear of heights and thus of flying, but ever since the September 11 attacks in New York and Washington, she'd been downright scared to death of flying. To make matters worse, just a few months ago she'd seen on the news that the Capital Records Tower in Los Angeles had been mentioned in some terrorist hit list – and she was flying into Los Angeles.

Jennie had spent a couple of hours the day before working with me on ways to manage her anxiety about the flight to LA, but now as she sat on her bed it was as if she knew nothing about anti-worry techniques. Her mind was a paralyzed amorphous mess, fixated only on her worst nightmare – of being in a hijacked jet heading directly toward the Capital Records Tower.

As she took a shower, she realized she was replaying this imaginary experience over and over in her mind, which of course was in turn directly stimulating her primitive fear system and provoking all manner of fear responses in her body. Finally, while drying off from the shower, she managed to gain some level of conscious control of her thoughts, as she began talking rationally to herself, remembering that her irrational worries had no basis in reality – that statistically the chance of her plane being hijacked or crashing into the ocean was vastly less than her car being in a fatal accident on the way to the airport. Furthermore, right now in this present moment, she wasn't even on a jet, so there was nothing to be immediately on fear alert about.

The rational thoughts helped somewhat, and she also remembered to turn her focus of attention to her breathing, which began to calm down, and to her heart, where she found some good feelings associated with visiting Peter's parents, whom she loved very much. Peter's father was just recovering from a minor operation, and it would be good to see him. She'd been so worried that something bad would happen to him in the hospital.

Peter was a great support through breakfast and as they drove down to the airport, reminding her of what they'd learned about anxiety control, and helping her to hold her mind on rational thoughts rather than drifting into worries, encouraging her to keep her focus in the present moment and enjoy the morning air and all the natural sights on their way to town.

But as they parked and walked to the air terminal, Jennie was again gripped by fear. Her mind kept leaping into the future and imagining being on the plane. She did her best to stay aware of her breathing in the present moment, and she kept telling herself that flying was the safest form of travel, even with the terrorist threats. Going through rigid security at the airport certainly didn't help her nerves, but she was managing to breathe and keep alert to her perceptions in the present moment. And Peter kept smiling and encouraging her.

Then they were walking down the corridor into the jet. Jennie could hardly feel her body, she was so afraid – she could almost directly experience the primitive fear system of her brain orchestrating a red-light emergency reaction – but she kept moving, telling herself that rationally there was nothing to fear at all, she wasn't going to die, she was jut going to go to Los Angeles and then return to Hawaii without incident.

They got to their seats and strapped in – and suddenly Jennie felt the utter terror of being completely helpless, a victim of whoever wanted to take over her life and . . . well, kill her. The jet engines started whining loudly outside the plane, and she felt the impulse to get up and start running, fighting anyone who tried to stop her from getting outside the airplane – but instead of acting out the impulse, she had to control her reflex to flee.

She could hear her mind screaming, "I'm going to die! I'm going to die!" and her imagination kept flashing the image of her plane crashing into the Capital Records Tower in a giant explosion of smoke and flame. And suddenly she remembered something I'd coached her on – that when she couldn't block an anxiety attack, it was best to surrender to it, to accept her worst imaginings and just let it play itself out to its grisly end. With no alternatives except to just pass out from the fear attack, spontaneously, she did just that. She stopped fighting her terror and let it consume her, as she imagined actually being hijacked, and then crashing into the tower and being killed instantly.

She felt the jet vibrating under her, and realized that they were taking off. But instead of still being frightened, she found her body was now strangely relaxed. She had imagined the worst, being killed outright – and something had let go in her, relaxed, accepted whatever might come. Here she was in flight, and instead of being scared out of her wits, she was just sitting in the plane, talking to Peter, almost feeling good in her body as the plane roared over the ocean.

"That was amazing," she confessed to Peter beside her. "Once I imagined the worst, being just smashed to smithereens and obliterated; the fear let go. That's me I guess – I'm not afraid to be dead, I'm just afraid of the moment when it happens. And right now, it's not happening. What a relief!"

When the pilot said to fasten seat belts for landing in Los Angeles, she did feel a sudden whole-body reflex as her mind again generated the vivid image of being right on the verge of crashing, the danger-alert image getting rushed to her primitive fear center, but instead of being overwhelmed with anxiety at the anticipation of her death, Jennie let the image go all the way again. And as soon as she imagined the crash itself and being obliterated and gone, she popped back into the present moment, because she'd defused the fear reaction by imagining the end actually happening, where the fear response makes no sense and is quiet.

They landed and Jennie was actually ebullient as they walked toward the baggage carrousel, feeling like she was somehow victorious, beyond the grip of her old fears. She knew she'd have to face the anxiety again on the trip home in four days, but she felt she'd conquered the problem – by facing death itself and calling its bluff.

Reeducating Your Amygdala

Jennie's account of her trip to LA highlights that there's no instant cure for deeply conditioned fears, especially those that border on phobia. Fear of heights is actually hardwired into our nervous system, so flying anxieties are especially difficult to deal with. That's why I used Jennie's story as an example – because it shows that even with a difficult fear, there are several ways we can act to at least reduce its severity and, in the long run, break free from its debilitating power.

I know that ever since I had Peter imagine the very worst happening to him, and especially after I had Jennie imagining her plane crashing, many of you are feeling uneasy about this whole technique. Who wants to imagine the worst? Don't we just program ourselves to have a terrible experience? Aren't we asking for disaster when we imagine the worst happening? And doesn't imagining the worst just condition our minds with more fear?

I thought the same when I did my initial therapy training with Dr. Charles Kelley of the Radix Institute, and he started guiding me into imagining all my worst fears. However, I quickly came to find that as soon as I'd imagined the worst, I was somehow set free from that chronic anxiety. The technique works – and works beautifully – to decondition ingrained fears.

But wait a minute. Why doesn't imagining something terrible happening just cause more anxiety? Key question, requiring further fine-tuning of our understanding of anxiety. When people worry about something terrible happening to someone, or to themselves, studies show that they never carry the imagination all the way through to the actual end of the disaster. They don't go all the way to the death in their imagination. Instead, they always stop halfway or three-fourths through the horrible imagination, and thus freeze themselves in fright. If they did move all the way through with their imagination, then the reverse would happen – they'd decondition the response, they'd free themselves from the fear. It's this freezing in fear halfway through the worried imagination that in essence blocks the deconditioning process. Please hold this in mind throughout this discussion.

Up until now I haven't raised the hoary issue of the psychological process called "conditioning" because the term tends to be associated primarily with rather low-level types of mental reprogramming. Indeed, the two primary psychological source books I recommended earlier in this chapter almost never use the term, preferring more fancy terminology and conceptualizations to the one we all learned in Psych 101.

However, I find it best to call a spade a spade, especially since within the basic paradigm of emotional conditioning we will discover a direct model for changing our fear patterns for the better. How do conditioning and deconditioning actually work? Here's an example, based on positive deconditioning, that should clarify the issue.

Imagine that you're quite young, and out of the blue, you get hit by a rock someone threw at you. The next time you see a rock flying at you, your amygdala will instantly process the visual data, remember that a similar situation caused great pain – and instantly activate your fear-duck response.

Meanwhile, even when there's no rock flying through the air at your head, sometimes your conscious mind remembers the experience of getting hit by the rock, and each time you remember the experience, you automatically run that memory-imagination through your amygdala – and it fires off a worried set of emotions related to getting hit by a rock.

All fine and good so far – you've experienced and been conditioned by a situation, and now you are programmed to react in such a way that you won't get hit in the head by the next rock thrown in your direction. In the same way, Jennie watched the World Trade Towers being destroyed by hijacked jet airliners, vicariously experienced the utter anguish of the victims of that disaster – and now whenever she even thinks of flying in an airliner, she gets hit with the seemingly wise fear reaction telling her, "No, that's dangerous, don't fly in jet airliners." Her conditioning to avoid pain and death is properly in place, but the conditioning might not be adequately defined and delineated. Unfortunately, as we've seen, the amygdala is not rational, and when conditioned by extreme emotions, it often has the power to overwhelm the rational fear center and plunge us into panic when panic is not truly called for.

How do we decondition the amygdala so that it responds with red-alert only in appropriate situations?

Let's consider the conditioned reflex to avoid getting hit in the head by a flying object. You turn 6 years old with this condition solidly in place, and suddenly get the urge to join your first baseball team, because your best friend has joined. You get out on the field, and all of a sudden people are throwing objects through the air at you – and you panic! Your primitive fear center is screaming, "Run for cover!" while your rational fear center is saying, "Cool it, this isn't dangerous, this is the name of the game."

The example is simple, yet the general situation is universal and applies to almost all our fear attacks. The early conditioning we received while growing up tends to be very general, often causing us to react to many situations with fear when in reality we're not endangered. In order to function successfully in society, we must learn to discriminate between genuinely dangerous situations and very similar situations that aren't dangerous at all. If we don't decondition our amygdala from reacting when we're not really in danger, we're going to live our lives as nervous, and unsuccessful, wrecks.

The exact same way you decondition your general fear of

flying objects so that you don't panic when someone throws you the baseball, is the way you decondition any fear – you put yourself in a learning situation where, over and over again, you experience the situation without anything bad happening to you. You play catch, and over and over again, you watch the ball flying toward you without hurting you. After a short while, your amygdala has learned through experience – it's become deconditioned (or "desensitized," as it's often called these days) so that it doesn't blow the panic whistle when you play baseball. Only when a ball comes too close to your head in a wild pitch, do you react with instant fear and duck. Otherwise, flying objects thrill you, they don't scare you.

Deconditioning a Fear Reaction

We've seen how we can decondition a prevailing anxiety by imagining the worst happening, and thus deconditioning the fear by accepting our own (or a friend's) death. This is the most extreme approach to anxiety deconditioning. There's another approach that works very well too, based on just the opposite approach: imagining over and over that you do something fearful, and nothing fearful happens. After a while, the fear becomes deconditioned based on the primary learning process of the mind.

Jennie got on the jet airliner full of fear that it would crash . . . and yet she flew to Los Angeles without incident. Nothing bad happened to her at all, even though her amygdala was conditioned to expect something bad to happen. Having such a safe experience in itself, will serve as a direct deconditioning process. If she flies often, she'll rapidly lessen her fear, all other things being equal.

Said simply: When, over and over again, something we expect to happen doesn't happen, we decondition our anticipation of that thing happening.

However, Jenny might not fly often enough to decondition the negative expectation. No problem – she can accelerate the deconditioning process considerably by using her memory and imagination to decondition her amygdala. Studies show that imagining a situation does impact our minds in similar ways to actually physically having the experience. Therefore, going back in memory and reliving her flight to Los Angeles over and over again, with absolutely nothing bad happening to her, will rapidly help Jennie decondition her general fear of flying in airplanes.

Here's the basic process. You can apply it to worries about your own well-being, and equally to worries about the well-being of people you love.

PAUSE AND EXPERIENCE
•

Make yourself comfortable . . . tune into your breathing . . . your heart . . . your whole body, here in this present moment . . . and now let your mind go back to an experience you had, where you felt afraid or threatened, in a particular situation that didn't really call for a fear reaction – where you were in no way threatened or harmed.

Remember the situation clearly . . . what you're doing, what you're seeing, what you're hearing around you . . . and because you know that you're not going to be hurt during the experience, instead of feeling fear in the situation, allow yourself to relax and feel safe and happy throughout the experience . . .

After you've relived the experience without feeling so much fear or no fear at all, say to yourself, "I'm not afraid of having that experience; I enjoy the experience."

Throughout the course of the day, turn your mind toward the experience or situation associated with fear, and remember your experience of being in the situation, and having nothing bad happen to you at all. In this way, actively decondition your mind from associating the situation with danger.

Time to Review

This chapter has covered several Ph.D.s' worth of insights into the nature and denaturing of a worried mind. Thanks for bearing with me. We had to think it all through from start to finish, in order to realistically understand how to quiet a worried mind. Obviously it's not a facile endeavor – fear is sticky stuff, even when it's inappropriate to the situation at hand. Once the amygdala has been convinced that a situation is dangerous to your well-being or even your very survival, it's sometimes darned difficult to convince it otherwise. But step-by-step, I assure you – you can.

Let's do a concise review of both the concepts and techniques we've learned in this chapter, in a short format you can return to whenever you're dealing with worries and want to quickly put your finger on the cure. Then we'll end with the primary guided session that takes you effortlessly through the de-worry procedure. Be sure to go through the process regularly in order to keep worries to a minimum.

1. We can worry about our own safety and well-being, or about the safety and well-being of another person. In either case, if

our thoughts chronically fixate on feared future scenarios, we can worry ourselves sick.

2. There are two primary types of fear that we experience: perceived danger in the present-moment environment and remembered or imagined danger in the past or future. Our primitive fear system serves us beautifully in dealing with present-moment environmental dangers. However, this same system can cause serious problems in our lives when we habitually project possible danger scenarios into the future, and generate a fear reaction in our bodies to this imagined danger – that is, when we worry too much.

3. When we react to a real or imagined life situation with fear, our bodies undergo an almost instantaneous hormonal, muscular, mental, and emotional transformation that prepares us either to aggressively do battle with the danger, or to rapidly run away and escape. This fear-transformation is excellent for dealing with environmental predators and other physical dangers; however, the same transformation can seriously undermine our performance and survival capabilities, not to mention our enjoyment of life, when the fight-flight charge is not released, but rather held in the body as long-term stress and anxiety.

4. There are two primary fear centers in the brain: the non-logical primitive-fear region called the amygdala and the more logical rational-fear region in the forebrain. The constant interaction of these two defense systems determines our present emotional mood, and our general success in negotiating the various challenges of life.

5. When we shift into fear mode, the dominant emotions we can feel are fright, rejection, repulsion, anger, aggression, helplessness, confusion, grief, or despair. When we're afraid, fear at least temporarily shuts down the more gentle relaxed

emotions such as compassion, joy, contentment, love, and bliss. At any given moment, we are either holding our systems in fear mode, or love mode – it's our ongoing choice.

6. Although the business world tends to operate on a high level of fear-based stress and aggression, worrying about one's business success actually undermines one's ability to perform optimally at work.

7. We can decondition our fearful expectations either through fully imagining the very worst all the way to the bloody end (to our death) or through remembering or imagining over and over, moving through an experience associated with fear, and experiencing no danger or harm at all.

8. Looking clearly at the present reality of a situation, and seeing that there is no longer danger related to the situation, will also help decondition the fear.

Whenever you find yourself worrying, at work or otherwise, there are five primary techniques to choose from, that you can apply to reduce or eliminate your anxieties, and thus quiet your mind for more enjoyable experiences. These five techniques are listed below, beginning with the process for dealing with mild worries, and then advancing into techniques for the more difficult anxieties. Apply these techniques regularly, to reduce your own worries.

De-Worry 1: Present-Moment Focusing

As we've seen, worrying about ourselves or those we love is the primary cause of an unquiet, disturbed state of consciousness. Worrying happens when the thinking mind keeps focusing on remembering something upsetting in the past, and then imagining something similar happening in the future. Worrying is thus a past-future function of the mind.

To actively decondition your habits of worrying overmuch about the future, regularly remember to pause once every fifteen minutes or half hour and do the basic two-minute meditation learned in the first chapter, to rapidly return your focus of attention to the quiet peace and intuitive clarity of the present moment.

1. Turn your mind's attention to the direct sensation of the air flowing in and out your nose.
2. Expand your awareness to include the movements in your chest and belly as you breathe.
3. Expand your awareness to also include your heart, right in the middle of your breathing.
4. Expand your awareness to include your whole body at once, here in the present moment.
5. Listen to the sounds around you . . . tune into the visual impressions coming to you . . . observe if there is any danger around you . . . and if not, relax completely and enjoy the present moment.

De-Worry 2: Observing Your Worry Habits

All too often, most of us go around habitually thinking worried thoughts and conjuring images about the future – rather than freeing our minds to perform more successfully and enjoy what's happening in the present moment. In order to free yourself from the habit of petty worrying, develop the positive habit of regularly stepping back from total immersion in your stream of thoughts, so that you can determine if your thoughts are fixated upon worrying.

If you observe that your mind is indeed locked in worries about the future, simply take note that you're doing this – catch yourself in the act. Quite often this will instantly stop the flow of worried thoughts and images and shift your focus of attention back to the present moment. Why? Because it feels good to be alive in the present moment. And it doesn't feel good to be dwelling on future worries that don't even exist.

Here's a self-reflection technique to help you develop this habit.

1. Remember to pause and observe the content of your thoughts.
2. Without being judgmental, just notice if you're worrying.
3. Whenever you find yourself worrying, choose to let go of the worries, and tune into the present moment.

This conscious act of regularly monitoring your thoughts for worry content can actively change your moment-to-moment experience dramatically. Worrying makes you feel bad – angry, depressed, suspicious, hopeless, weak, confused, apprehensive. As soon as you catch your mind in worry mode and shift away from the past-future into the present moment, your mood will respond accordingly by becoming brighter, more heart-centered, spontaneous, joyful, and creative. You naturally prefer pleasure to pain, so you'll condition your mind to stay out of worry mode.

De-Worry 3: Calling Worry's Bluff

When monitoring your thoughts and consciously shifting into the present moment to quiet your worries doesn't work adequately, then it's time to more actively put your worries to rest. Very often your fears are irrational, which means they are not based on the reality of the situation. Somewhere in your past, you developed a general fear reaction to a situation, and even though the situation has changed, you haven't updated your beliefs and assumptions to correct an outdated fear association.

Whenever you find yourself worrying, pause long enough to ask yourself the following questions, and see if the fear is even valid. If you call its bluff and use reason to show that the fear isn't really applicable to your present situation, the worry will be directly defused. This is a process where we actually use the cognitive thinking mind to defuse old unrealistic fears, so that the mind can relax.

- What are you afraid might happen?
- In the light of reason, is this really a valid fear?
- Do you need to keep this fear to get along well in life?
- How would your life change if you let go of this fear?

If you discover that the assumptions underlying the anxiety are valid, then definitely, remain alert to the danger involved. However, if you find that the assumptions are no longer valid, replace them with more realistic assumptions.

Important: Regularly vocalize and imagine your new assumptions, so that the amygdala "hears" the new information, and forms new response paradigms to that situation. For instance, you might say to yourself, "I don't have to be so afraid when I'm in a group situation like this. I'm mature and can take care of myself. There's nothing dangerous here, and I'm not afraid anymore." Or: "The world's not going to end if I lose this job. I'm competent, I work hard, and I can always get another job."

De-Worry 4: Looking to the Source

Sometimes we're so anxious that our minds are constantly full of worrying thoughts, leaving no peace at all inside our own heads. If the first de-worry techniques didn't work for you, perhaps it is necessary to face head-on the underlying but often mostly unconscious core fear that is chronically provoking all manner of surface worries. The following process involves imagining the very worst – and in so doing, facing your own death, and thus learning to accept whatever comes into your life without apprehension.

1. State the worry that's gripping you: What is the present or future situation that you're anxious about?

2. In your mind's imagination, explore the worst possible scenario to the ultimate limit: What are you really afraid might happen if all your worst fears were to come true?

3. Accept whatever experiences that fate might bring you in the future. Ultimately, imagine and then accept your own eventual death.

4. Now, having imagined the worst, reflect and consider if your present reason for worrying is realistic. Is your worst possible scenario really what would happen to you, or is your fearful imagination exaggerating reality?

5. Realize that your chronic worrying about a possible future event is causing you immediate suffering in the present moment, and therefore not a healthy or loving thing to do to yourself.

6. Once you've seen that your worried thoughts don't reflect reality and are causing you to suffer, choose to move entirely beyond past-future mental games and shift into present-moment enjoyment. Focus on the sensory experiences coming to you in the present moment. You're no longer being plagued by worries, and therefore you're free to be fully "here."

De-Worry 5: Deconditioning the Fear Response

Worries are conditioned responses that you learned in your past, that you are transposing and projecting into the future and upsetting yourself with. Often, the best way to get rid of a chronic anxiety that isn't rationally valid, is to decondition the fear response directly. This is done by putting yourself in the fear-inducing situation over and over, either in reality or in your imagination, and experiencing nothing bad happening to you. Through this process, you successfully decondition the negative reaction to the situation.

1. Recognize that you are feeling anxious in situations that are no longer a threat to your well-being, and that this anxiety is disturbing your ability to enjoy the present moment.
2. Consciously put yourself in the anxiety-causing situation over and over again, and stay aware of the reality that nothing dangerous or hurtful happens to you in this situation.
3. After each deconditioning experience, reflect upon the experience, and tell your worry center that there is no need to react with anxiety in such situations.

You can also perform this deconditioning process by remembering experiences where you were in the fearful situation and nothing bad happened to you, or by imagining being in the situation and having a positive experience. Hold regularly in mind that you can unlearn a fear reaction in the same way as you learned it – if you consciously apply this deconditioning technique in one form or another.

The choice is always yours: to continue focusing on all your worries (past-future mentation) or to choose to focus on accepting life and taking whatever comes (present-moment awareness). Worrying always involves a noisy thinking mind. Quieting your mind silences your worries.

Here's a guided session to help you make the shift from chronic worrying to inner peace, taking you effortlessly through the basic processes learned in this chapter. I strongly recommend that you do this session at least once a week, to decondition old worry habits and to catch any new anxieties that might be gaining a subtle grip on your soul.

GUIDED SESSION 3:

SILENCING CHRONIC WORRIES

•

Set aside ten to fifteen minutes free from outside bothers, and make yourself comfortable . . . stretch a little if you want to . . . yawn and sigh perhaps . . . maybe massage your face and hands gently . . .

And now tune into your breathing . . . your heart . . . your toes . . . your fingers . . . your pelvis . . . your whole body, here in this present moment . . .

Now, begin to remember something that you've been worrying about . . . something terrible or unacceptable that you're concerned might happen to you, emotionally or physically, sometime in the uncertain future . . .

What are you afraid might happen? Say your fear to yourself: "I'm afraid that _____." Now imagine what you're afraid of, actually happening to you . . . experience one of your worst fears actually happening to you . . . breathe into the experience . . . go all the way . . . What really is your core fear in life, the one that underlies all your worries? What are you afraid will happen to you?

Now, in the light of reason, let's consider the initial worry that's been plaguing you. Is this really a valid fear? Considering your life as a whole, is what you worry about happening, besides your ultimate death of course, really going to happen to you, or is it just one of many possibilities of your unborn future?

Quietly ask yourself these questions: "Do I really need to keep this fear of future danger activated by worrying in order to get along well in life?" "Is it necessary to keep imagining something bad happening to me in the future, in order for me to keep myself safe in the unfolding present moment?" "Does worrying help me by keeping me anxious all the time, or does worrying actually get in the way of dealing successfully with challenges?"

How would your life change, if you let go of this particular recurrent worry? What would happen to you, if you stopped worrying altogether? How would your body feel, if you let go of this worry?

Imagine that you're now in the general situation that you're afraid might hurt or damage you at some point in the future. Imagine that whatever the danger or threat, you meet this danger successfully, and survive, even positively thrive in the situation . . .

Now imagine that you're once again in a similar situation that you used to worry about happening. Imagine that once again, you live through the situation without being hurt in any way . . . that you actually enjoy the situation . . .

Now, bring to mind something else that you worry about, this time about something happening to someone you love. First, imagine the very worst thing happening . . . let your worst nightmare for this person's future run through your mind . . . experience even their terrible death . . .

Now, let go of that worry, and imagine them in the same situation, doing perfectly well, dealing successfully with the danger at hand . . . even thriving in the situation and having a good time . . .

Again, does worrying about someone you love ever help them? Do you do them a service imagining terrible things happening to them, or do you help them in their life by imagining them succeeding in dangerous situations, and being victorious when challenged?

Say to yourself, "I want to stop worrying about the future."

"I am letting go of my fears, and accepting whatever comes."

"I accept whatever comes —and choose to live life fully in the present moment."

Now just relax. Tune into your breathing . . . your heart . . . and say to yourself, "My heart is open, to receive . . . to accept . . . to embrace the present moment without fear."

As the music plays, enjoy living right here, right now . . . without any worries running through your mind . . . trusting the present moment . . . enjoying life to the fullest . . .

For streamed-audio guidance through this experience, go to www.johnselby.com.

chapter 4

listening to your heart

We all learned while growing up that silence is golden, that people listen when we speak from the heart, that love makes the world go around. We might even have been told in a Sunday school class to memorize the saying of Jesus where he stated in unequivocal terms the spiritual equation that "God is love." Everywhere we might turn in our society, love has been an active ingredient in how people think about themselves and each other, and how they relate to themselves and each other. Every religion in the world is built upon the underlying premise that at the very center of our personal experience is a unique feeling found only in the heart, a feeling called love.

This chapter is dedicated to perhaps the deepest reward to be gained through mastering a quiet mind, the remarkable changes that come on all levels – biological, psychological, emotional, and spiritual – when you learn to regularly enter into a state of cognitive silence and focus your mind's attention on the pure essence of love and peace found at the center of your being, directly within your physical heart.

But how does a commonplace biological pump performing a basic muscular task somehow attain such a lofty status as the spiritual container of the most elusive yet most pervading and certainly most desired experience of the human race, that of love itself?

A couple of decades ago, I would have had to answer that question purely in esoteric and subjective terminology. However, the last twenty years of research in neurocardiology have transformed this discussion. Based on research initiated by John and Beatrice Lacey at the National Institute of Health and advanced considerably at other research centers, we now know that along with all its muscular and connective tissue, somewhere between 60 and 65 percent of all the cells in your heart are actually neurons exactly like those in your brain. Furthermore, there exist intensive unmediated neural connections between the emotional limbic region of the brain and the heart, such that "tremendous interaction occurs between the heart and the emotional brain." Furthermore, the neural cells in the heart communicate with each other through the same neural transmitters, the same type of dendrites and axons, as they do in the brain. Likewise the heart's neural ganglia produce the same hormones as those produced in the brain.

In sum, although this may sound quite startling, the heart organ is beginning to be perceived by the more advanced neurologists as "the fifth brain," along with the four brains (reptilian, mammalian, forebrain, and prefrontal lobes) we find working together in the cranium. Research even demonstrates that the heart produces hormones that influence performance of the brain. In fact, at least half of the neurons of the heart have been found to be connected to, and to influence, the major organs of the body.

What does this mean, that the heart is the fifth brain of the human organism? And how does this fifth brain interact with, and influence, the rest of the mind and body? Recent studies of conception and the first weeks of life in the womb show that the first brain to develop is indeed the heart, and that the tiny heart seems to begin beating in direct interaction with the heartbeat of the mother. A powerful entrainment happens so that there is a scientifically observable pulsative harmony between the mother and the fetal heart. Indeed, a controversy presently exists concerning the possibility that the fetal heart begins beating not from orders from its own brain (hardly present at this point at the top of the nervous system) but from an energetic entrainment with the electromagnetic force field of the mother's heart.

Another distinct body of research has been developing that demonstrates that the human heart is indeed a powerful electromagnetic generator. Already, scientific instruments have documented that the heart produces a three-phase electromagnetic force field that radiates at least fifteen feet beyond the body – and probably indefinitely beyond that. Our heart is, in other words, a powerful broadcast transmitter, influencing the fetal heart and surely interacting with the electromagnetic force field of other peoples' hearts. This is actual energy being broadcast, and the magnitude of the energy is a full forty times greater than the total magnitude of the brain's energy.

Science identifies many different types of electromagnetic fields. Current research is exploring the implications of the experimental observation that the type of force field being broadcast by the human heart is the same as (although of course vastly smaller than) the electromagnetic force field of our planet. This particular type of force field, called the "torus field" by mathematicians and physicists, is considered in general to be the most stable form of energy known in the universe. Furthermore, the same type of torus electromagnetic radiation field is also found around the sun itself, and around our entire solar system. In the other direction, molecules are also grounded in the torus energy format.

As Joseph Chilton Pierce explains it, "The torus energy field of our heart is in effect a nested hierarchy in a nested hierarchy of electro-magnetic fields." And naturally one begins to wonder if the pulsation of a fetus's heart is entrained not only in harmony with its mother's heart but with the energetic pulsation of its planet and its sun.

At this point, the emerging scientific view of the heart becomes almost mystical in stature, such that each heartbeat, with its resulting wave of electromagnetic energy, possesses the broadcast power capable of carrying an almost infinite amount of information – the equivalent of 1,500 cycles on your radio or television. And each broadcast of each heartbeat sends out information that interacts with the information being broadcast by the radiation fields of the planet and the solar system. As the Chinese biologist May Wan Ho at London University puts it, "Each heart is in essence the heart of the universe. Our individual heart is connected with whatever there is everywhere." Scientifically, there is only one universal heart, within which our individual hearts beat.

Heart and Brain

The four brains in the top of our head and the brain in the center of our chest are connected through the spine with a major assortment of two-way neural pathways. We're only beginning to comprehend exactly how these neurological centers communicate and influence each other. However, here's a fact of high import: Neurological studies show that the heart is connected primarily not to the rational verbal frontal region of our cranium but to the older emotional limbic region and to the perceptual regions of the brain.

When our perceptual system receives sensory information from the outside world, processes that information and compares it with similar previous experience that evoked a particular emotion, the result of this associative memory search is communicated immediately to the neural consciousness of the heart.

Right at this point, the process shifts from being just a perception or an idea about the outside world into an actual feeling, a definite physiological phenomenon that "moves" us emotionally. How does this actual feeling – for instance, of compassion – manage to come into being? Through the heart's orchestration of a host of physiological changes that occur in the heart itself – as muscles contract or relax, hormones surge or diminish, and messages get sent to other parts of the body to respond physiologically – so we experience a whole-body physical feeling associated with the experience before us.

Meanwhile, sensory nerves throughout the body report this physiological change back to the conscious brain upstairs, indicating that an emotional feeling is occurring. Thus we can look at the face of someone we have felt love for in the past, and immediately our associative powers go to work that remember feelings we've had in our heart for this person before. This emotional pattern is communicated to our heart, which goes through its physiological changes to generate the actual emotion again.

So finally, here we have the scientific model describing how our hearts "feel" our emotions physically. Furthermore there is considerable data now in, showing that the conversation runs both ways. The limbic system sends the heart a basic report on associative past experiences, and at the same time sends the logical thinking brain this information, as we've seen before. Then something truly mysterious happens – a flow of neurological information flows from the heart-brain to the frontal lobes, stimulating responses in the brain itself.

The heart seems to process sensory and associative information, and then send information and also action orders to the brain, exactly as if the heart functions as a conscious intelligent participant in the decision-making process. We're just barely on the edge of understanding this heart-brain decision-making process, but the indicators are present that the heart is indeed an equal participant in our decisions and resulting actions.

One further bit of valuable information: The thinking mind on its own, without any perceptual stimulation from the outside world, can think a thought about someone or some situation, such as "Ah, I sure do love Jeffrey," and the thought will stimulate related memories and fantasies, and these together will flood the heart with emotionally laden content, which will provoke a physiological feeling of love throughout the body. In fact, probably most of the emotional stimulation that the heart feels, for most of us, is generated not by present-moment encounters but by rerunning past encounters through the mind and heart.

Of course, the heart also can feel very painful negative emotions stimulated by the thinking mind, as we've seen already. If our minds are fixated upon worries, the heart will contract with its usual defensive compassion-shut-down reaction in the presence of danger. Likewise, if angry thoughts are chronically dominating our thoughts, our hearts will be hit with angry feelings. In this light, this whole book thus far has been an exploration of how our thoughts force our hearts into painful emotions or encourage our hearts to sing with positive feelings.

However, we've also seen that there's another entirely different realm of experience for the human organism – when we quiet our minds tune into the present moment and let the heart respond directly to the experiences coming to our senses in the here and now. Only when we liberate the heart from past-fixated preprogrammed emotions, can the heart truly participate as a conscious presence that not only responds to thoughts and memories but also responds spontaneously "from the heart" to new experiences. And this is the realm where life becomes truly transcendent and heartwarming.

Let's do a simple experiment in this regard, using your own inner experience as the lab. Notice as clearly as you can exactly what happens within you when you do the following.

PAUSE AND EXPERIENCE

•

After reading this paragraph, close your eyes, tune into your breathing . . . the feelings (if any right now) in your heart . . . your whole-body presence here in the present moment . . . and without effort, allow the face of someone you love, to come to mind . . . open your heart to this person by saying "I love you" and notice what actual physical changes happen inside your own heart . . .

Whole-Body Consciousness

We are just emerging from a period of history where the Age of Reason so dominated our general attitudes that we taught our young to trust their nonemotional deductive reasoning powers when making a decision in life, to the specific exclusion of their heart-based emotional feelings. It has been considered quite foolish to "lead with the heart" rather than the head. And indeed, as long as we're mismanaging our minds so that the heart is forced to simply reproduce emotions based on past experience, it's best to employ deductive logic in making a decision.

But as we come to perceive the heart as a large and energetically very powerful brain capable of its own unique form of perception and communication, we're now at the point where we need to reassess our entire cultural attitude about the heart. And the story doesn't end with the heart either – research has documented that the largest organ of our body, our own skin, is also made up of a vast array of brain neurons that can readily be seen as the sixth brain of our body. When you take the vast surface area of the skin and make it into a ball, it's actually a larger neural presence than the brain itself. And who knows what unique consciousness this massive neural configuration might possess.

In the other direction, each of the billions of cells throughout our bodies can be observed very clearly performing as a unique individual conscious entity in rather perfect entrainment with all other cells of the body – generating the conscious whole. Joseph Chilton Pierce explains this phenomenon clearly in his book *Magical Child:* "Intelligence is not assigned only to the brain and nervous system," says Pierce. "Every cell of our bodies is an intelligence of staggering complexity, and every cell acts intelligently. . . . All the basic functions needed for the human body to thrive – movement, nutrition, elimination, reproduction, awareness, and yes, even intelligence – are found in every living cell. Each cell contains a pattern of the whole. Intelligence is everywhere and we are that intelligence."

However, we've seen that if we mismanage our minds, if we let preprogrammed reactions and beliefs and assumptions and thoughts determine our behavior, we effectively shut down most of our whole-body consciousness and get stuck in a past-future internal feedback loop of thought and resulting emotion that separates us from the true learning zone – the perceptual present moment.

When you habitually lose awareness of your breathing, your heart, your whole body here in this present moment, you are basically short-circuiting the basic learning function of the human organism. Learning, after all, is defined as an ongoing unique interaction between your past experience (memory and conditioning) with new inputs from the present-moment world around you. And only by shifting your focus of attention in perceptual directions can you reactivate your learning capacity, where your whole organism experiences the world around you, and responds appropriately. Otherwise you tend to go through life mostly out of touch both with the learning opportunities coming to you and with the vast intelligence and loving power of your own heart and whole body... with your seemingly infinite realms of wisdom and primal connectedness with the world.

When you establish new mental habits of regularly pausing and tuning into your heart and whole-body presence, you almost instantly awaken a wisdom and palpable power grounded in an integrative intelligence far beyond your deductive processes – in fact grounded in the ultimate wisdom and harmonic power of the universe itself.

The great German philosopher, scientist, and educator Rudolf Steiner, almost a century ago, taught that the heart is intelligent, intimately linked with the brain, and most importantly, possessed of a quality of intelligence that transcends the other mental capacities of the brain. For him, as for a great many spiritual masters before him, the heart is our true teacher. Joseph Chilton Pierce, one of Steiner's strongest adherents, puts it so succinctly: "The greatest challenge we face is to allow the heart, which is really the heart of the universe, to speak."

This chapter is dedicated to exploring the best way for you to redirect your mind's habitual focus of attention, and tap into your heart's intelligence, so that right in the center of cognitive silence, you tune into what your greater wisdom and ultimately the universe and beyond has to say to you, moment to moment. Twenty years ago, such a statement would have been considered esoteric. Now we have renowned scientists, with evidence in hand, saying the same thing – the heart is a primal ingredient in human consciousness, the heart is connected electromagnetically with other people and ultimately with the entire universe and its vast intelligence. Each of us can tune into this intelligence through a simple shift of our attention's focus.

PAUSE AND EXPERIENCE
•

Again, let's do it rather than just talk about it. Even while reading these evocative words, expand your awareness to include the experience of the air rushing in and out your nose (or mouth) as you breathe . . . and expand your awareness another step to also include the effortless movements of your chest and belly as you breathe . . . and expand your awareness to also include your heart, right in the middle of your breathing . . . and now be aware of your whole body, here in this present moment . . . and be open to a unique heartfelt experience . . .

Loving Yourself

As the old song says, "Everybody loves a lover," and this is certainly true. When our hearts are open, when we're not judging other people but accepting them just as they are, their hearts in turn actually receive this energetic broadcast from our hearts, and are encouraged to entrain with our good heart feelings and respond in kind. We spread love, we amplify good feelings, by nurturing love in our hearts – and sharing that love freely wherever we go. It's that simple, really.

You have your own group of friends, relatives, colleagues, however large or small. And at the center of your own being, you also have your own relationship with your self. Over the years you've naturally developed all sorts of opinions about each of your friends, and about yourself as well. And you will notice that you go about each new day sometimes fairly open with your love, and sometimes quite closed off from feeling any compassion at all.

A primary aim of this chapter is simply to encourage you to begin noticing, each and every moment if possible, how you are relating "heart-wise" to the world around you, and to your own self. In any given moment and situation, is your mind quiet of defensive or worried judgments and your heart therefore open, or is your mind almost constantly judging yourself and the people around you, and in so doing, closing down your ability to share good heart feelings?

It's important, as we begin this self-reflective process related to your openness to love, that you don't judge yourself if you discover that your current habits are quite full of judgment, and your heart therefore very often closed to acceptance and love. Remember what we've learned earlier, that the very act of seeing that you are holding your heart closed to someone will help to open your heart to that person. And this certainly applies to your love for yourself as well.

We saw earlier that most of us tend to judge our own selves habitually and quite harshly, usually based on unquestioned negative assumptions and beliefs picked up in early childhood about our basic sense of self-worth, lovability, and capacity to take care of ourselves successfully.

What about your present ability, or lack thereof, to love yourself just as you are? How do you judge yourself, day in and day out? Let's take time now to bring your habits of self-rejection or self-acceptance to the surface. By bringing these judgmental habits into conscious awareness, you will spontaneously begin to transcend them.

To help you with this task, I've listed eight statements that describe your feelings about some key aspect of your self-image. The statements are on a scale ranging from 1 (most positive) to 10 (most negative). Before you react and evaluate each response, pause and close your eyes for a moment, tune into a full breath cycle, expand to include your heart, and in this state of inner silence, open your eyes, look again and read the statement. Then honestly rate yourself according to how you feel about yourself *right now.* Don't get upset if you find that you're judging yourself at less than optimum levels. Simply acknowledge your present attitude toward yourself based on past conditioning, knowing that this negative self-judgment can be readily changed through the techniques we're learning in this book. If you find that you are judging yourself fairly harshly, I recommend that you do this five-minute exercise once a day for a week to stimulate deep reflection and growth.

SELF-JUDGMENT REFLECTION

1. "I look okay"   "I look terrible"
   1   2   3   4   5   6   7   8   9   10

2. "I trust other people"   "People can't be trusted"
   1   2   3   4   5   6   7   8   9   10

3. "I'm smart enough"   "I'm not smart enough"
   1   2   3   4   5   6   7   8   9   10

4. "I feel safe"   "I'm in danger"
   1   2   3   4   5   6   7   8   9   10

5. "I'm a good person"   "I'm a bad person"
   1   2   3   4   5   6   7   8   9   10

6. "I can take care of myself"   "I'm helpless"
   1   2   3   4   5   6   7   8   9   10

7. "Life is great"   "Life is terrible"
   1   2   3   4   5   6   7   8   9   10

8. "I'm entirely lovable"   "I'm totally unlovable"
   1   2   3   4   5   6   7   8   9   10

When you consider each of these statements, always be honest about your feelings in the moment. These beliefs exist inside your mind right now – they're real. Accept them, knowing you can change them for the better through conscious action.

Once you've done this initial detective work on your hidden self-judgments, once you've identified an area of low self-esteem where you're judging yourself as not worthy, as unlovable, as helpless, you can use the de-beliefing process you learned in Chapter 2 to explore your self-judgment and determine if it is true in the light of present reason.

Also, hold in mind that regardless of how the rest of the world might judge you, you have the freedom to see yourself positively. This can be a truly enlightening experience. I once worked as a group therapy leader at San Quentin prison with a group of nine inmates who had all murdered at least one person. I was certainly challenged at first not to judge these people as bad, untrustworthy, stupid, dangerous, unlovable – and of course, they were judging themselves mostly the same way. But after two or three months of more and more honest communication, plus the employment of techniques similar to what you find in this book, an amazing change had come over all of us. We had processed our negative judgments of ourselves, and watched as others processed their negative judgments, and we'd all experienced a transformation of our judgments of each other, for the better.

What we found was that when we risked opening our hearts to love ourselves and each other without judgment, love flowed in, transformation occurred, self-images brightened, and souls came back to life.

When we include the heart factor, when we allow the intelligence and wisdom and healing power of the heart to actively influence our experience of who we are, everyone on this planet is lovable. We can all be trustworthy. After all, within the power of love, we are all perfect in the eyes of God. We live in a perfect universe, and we're an integral part of this universe. Our hearts when allowed to, beat in harmony and entrainment with the love that pervades physical creation . . . and unless we judge ourselves as otherwise, we are indeed entirely okay, just as we are. However far we may have fallen in society's eyes, when we accept ourselves, and open our hearts to healing and guidance, we can begin anew and live a new life grounded in love.

You'll discover through experiment and experience that when you come to feel this deep resonating quality of self-acceptance in your own heart, you will spontaneously heal emotionally, as you naturally let go of the negative, damaging beliefs that have been dragging you down.

In the act of seeing yourself as lovable, you become lovable. The eight paired statements I just gave you to reflect upon represent a primary tool for you to use over and over so that you progressively advance into a brighter self-image. For each statement that you do not score as a 1, ask yourself the following questions. Take time to explore the belief that underlies your self-judgment, and, step-by-step, let go of your negative feelings toward yourself.

1. Where did this negative attitude toward myself come from?
2. Am I sure my negative self-judgment is true?
3. How does it influence my life, believing that the negative statement is true?
4. When I look at the positive statement, and say it to myself, how do I feel?
5. In what ways would my life change, if I just let go of this negative attitude toward myself?

Your attitude toward yourself – in fact, your entire self-image – is purely a product of your past, not your present. When you live in thoughts and memories and conditioned reactions, you remain stuck in the past and a victim of whatever negative experiences have come your way. Why? Because you can't change the past, no matter how much you think about it and agonize over it and condemn it and wish you'd done otherwise.

The only thing you can do to free yourself from negative self-judgments based on the past is to just let go of it all and focus on the unique unfolding of your always-new present moment – by doing exactly what we learned in Chapter 1: regularly quieting the flow of thoughts (the past intruding upon the present moment) through your mind, tuning into the wisdom and love emanating from your heart, and living within the embrace of the experiences coming to you right now.

When you are living in the present moment, how you feel right now determines who you are, not what you felt or did or had done to you in the past. And right now, nothing stands between you and total loving acceptance of yourself and the world around you, except your own judgmental function of your mind. Ultimately, learning to love requires nothing more than just taking the leap and doing it, accepting yourself as okay just as you are, and opening up to the presence of your heart so that you let the love flow.

PAUSE AND EXPERIENCE

•

After reading this paragraph, close your eyes for a few moments, and simply turn your focus of attention toward your own heart experience . . . it doesn't matter for now if your heart feels good or bad, hurt or happy, open or closed . . . what matters is that you begin to hold your attention, more and more, focused on your heart . . . so that change and learning can happen, as the warmth of your own mind's attention soothes your heart . . . love yourself enough to give your own heart nonjudgmental loving attention . . .

Giving and Receiving

Everyone talks about the power of love, and the interaction of two hearts in love. Obviously love is more than an idea – we feel impacted by love, we feel immersed in it, we feel touched by other hearts. We saw earlier in this chapter that science has now documented how energetic emanations from the human heart radiate outward around the body. I'd like to briefly share with you additional research in a related field, that verifies and clarifies the impact of the human heart-mind on the outside world.

Perhaps you've already heard about the Princeton Studies in Applied Consciousness, which have recently demonstrated even beyond a skeptic's doubt that human beings do "touch" each other directly when they focus their attention on each other. If this material is already part of your scientific understanding, feel free to jump quickly beyond this short section.

However, if you're not familiar specifically with the Princeton Engineering Anomalies Research Project carried out under the guidance of Professor Robert Jahn, you should find the following paragraphs highly interesting, as they describe seminal research that will rapidly impact our basic worldview about the verifiable power of the human heart-mind to impact and communicate from a distance.

The issue of direct transpersonal communication is of course not a new one. Throughout history, many of our wisest scholars and scientists have openly claimed that they could sense the presence of an invisible yet almost palpable power within their own minds. Isaac Newton, that patriarch of classic Western science, stated that the primary force of change in the world would prove to be "the mystery by which mind could control matter." Francis Bacon, father of the experimental method, was highly interested in studying such "mind over matter" phenomena as telepathic dreams, psychic healing, transmission of spirits, and the power of the mind on the casting of dice. And in contemporary physics, Max Planck, Neils Bohr, Albert Einstein, Werner Heisenberg, Erwin Schroedinger, and David Bohm have all written about the still-mysterious influence of consciousness on external matter and events.

However, only recently has our experimental method become technologically sharp enough to test once and for all the driving question of whether or not the human heart and mind can broadcast actual energetic information beyond the physical body. The last twenty years have been landmark decades for consciousness research. Any number of studies could be cited from around the world, but perhaps the first and by now most solid set of studies demonstrating the specific impact of the mind on the environment and other people is that begun in 1979 by Robert Jahn, noted professor of aerospace sciences and dean of the traditionally quite conservative Princeton School of Engineering and Applied Science. Jahn established the Princeton Engineering Anomalies Research Center for "the scientific study of consciousness-related physical phenomena."

Intending to finally prove or disprove Francis Bacon's early questioning of whether our mind can influence the tossing of dice, the flipping of coins, and other supposedly random phenomena, the following experimental situation was set up at Princeton:

Using the most sensitive data systems available, a human operator would sit with a computer that was randomly generating either "plus" (+1) or "minus" (-1) signs at a very rapid rate. The operator's instructions were very simple – to employ his or her willpower, or power of intent, to influence the statistically random output of the computer.

Note that no differentiation was made in this study between cranial brain power and cardiac heart power. From what we now know about the heart being an integral part of the

brain system of the body, we can assume that the heart's energetic radiation was a factor in the "power of intent" in the
experiment.

In each test run, a naive "general population" operator was
asked first to focus his or her attention toward helping the
computer generate the expected "zero" total of the +1 and -1
random output. On the second run the operator was asked
to employ his or her conscious intent, in helping the computer to generate a "higher than expected" numerical output.
Then on the third run the operator was asked to focus on influencing the computer to generate a "lower than expected"
numerical output.

From the classic Western scientific understanding, there
should have been statistically zero difference between the three
runs. But the opposite proved true: "The overall results indicate a modest but persistent achievement that is well beyond
any reasonable chance expectation." The experiment was run
literally thousands of times to make sure the results were statistically valid.

The results remained statistically significant. Somehow the
human mind was able to influence the performance of a machine, purely through conscious present-moment mental-
emotional intent.

Once the initial Princeton study data was compiled and
processed showing that the human mind can influence a computer that is spatially close to the operator, the designers of the
Human/Machine Interaction Study decided to see if the power
of consciousness over matter remains the same or diminishes
over space.

They began separating human from machine with ever-
increasing distances, looking for the anticipated dropoff effect
over distance. However, much to their surprise, they didn't

find any dropoff at all. Even when the operator was thousands of miles from the machine (Princeton to Tokyo), the ability to positively or negatively influence the random output of the machine remained unchanged. Distance was clearly not a variable in the consciousness equation. Here was yet another anomaly that flew in the face of conventional scientific thinking – yet one that makes perfect sense when lovers claim that they are in intimate touch with each other, no matter how far apart they might be on the planet.

Almost surely, Professor Jahn and his associates concluded, the actual broadcast coming from the human mind must be some kind of wave pattern, traveling through some as-yet-unidentified medium. At this point the researchers got really nervy. They decided to go ahead and study the variable of time in their experimental model by having the operator broadcast his intent to the machine a specified amount of time (ranging up to 336 hours) before the machine would be turned on.

Again, truly startling results were obtained. The factor of time between stimulus and response didn't diminish the operator's mental ability to influence the random output of the machine. Somehow the medium through which the conscious intent was broadcast had stored this information until the computer was turned on and the study run.

The Princeton studies came upon yet another rather astounding statistic, very close to our present theme of the heart being an active ingredient in the consciousness equation. When operators were paired in the research, directing their intent as a two-person team toward the functioning of the machine, these pairs repeatedly yielded startling positive results – with average effects *3.7 times greater* than those of a single operator.

This discovery clearly indicates that when two heart-minds are put together, this union of intent somehow amplifies the results gained. And if all this isn't enough, here's yet another key discovery emerging from the Princeton studies: when opposite-sex pairs who were romantically bonded (married or girlfriend-boyfriend) with a strong emotional love relationship worked together as a team, their results were "nearly *six times* those of the single operators."

There's no way around this statistic. The research team ran a great many tests to be sure they were statistically and experimentally valid, and over and over, they found that the simple procedure of bringing emotional love into the picture increased the positive results of "mind over matter" to really quite startling proportions.

In addition to all this research, in equally radical experiments the Princeton study group documented, for the first time to the satisfaction of even the most skeptical scientists, that two friends can communicate both symbols and visual images to each other over any distance and beyond the confines of linear time. Purely through the mysterious power of two empathetic heart-minds in positive emotional resonance with each other, detailed communication can be broadcast and received between distant human bodies, through as-yet-unknown processes and mediums.

Considering all this startling data input, Professor Jahn and his associates at Princeton have now concluded, after twenty years of exploring what they term the "consciousness/environment interaction" phenomenon, that there exists no distinct boundary between mind and matter at the wave-particle level of reality. Instead, writes Jahn, "consciousness is allowed to permeate outward into its surrounding environment to an extent consistent with its prevailing purpose."

And so we now have this scientific evidence indicating that yes, individual human consciousness does impact its environment, and that emotional love is an active ingredient. What does this mean specifically in the context of our discussion? First of all, the thoughts we think are not only influencing our own inner realms, they're also impacting the people around us. The machines that were influenced by human intent in the Princeton studies were gross compared to the human brain, so we can expect a much higher level of impact, brain to brain, than brain to machine.

When we broadcast fearful or judgmental thoughts, these thoughts are being received by other human beings, regardless of distance and time. So every time we slip into fear-based thoughts, we're broadcasting fear throughout the world. At this level indeed, our business gets broadcast into everyone else's business. When we indulge in fear-based thinking and imaginings, we're impacting the whole world.

Conversely, and here's the good news, when we silence such fear-inducing thoughts, and tune into the natural peace and love within our own hearts, we radiate this love demonstrably out to the world. This is perhaps the scientific explanation of how people still feel the love of Buddha or Mohammed or Jesus strongly in their hearts, even many centuries after their physical presence has left the earth. When we open our hearts to receive love, we indeed do experience love rushing into our hearts – from all the love that has and will be generated by loving hearts.

And so we come to see, even from a scientific perspective, the great value in regularly pausing to silence our thinking minds, tune into our whole-body presence, open our hearts and both receive and share with the world around us the seemingly infinite power of love that abides eternally in the hearts of us all – if we choose to welcome its presence in our lives.

The tools now exist, as we've learned, to deal effectively

with the judgments and fears, programmed beliefs and reactions that hold us in fear, and therefore out of love. In these four chapters we've covered the basic theory and practice of these "quiet your mind" techniques. I'm also offering you ongoing online audio guidance and an ever-expanding community to nurture quiet minds and open hearts (www.john selby.com). You have what you need to succeed in quieting your mind and opening your heart.

But – What If Your Heart Hurts?

All along, I've been encouraging you to turn your focus of attention to your heart. Surely the basic idea is sound, and the positive intent quite clear by now. All our good feelings are felt in the heart, so if we want to enjoy life, if we want to fill our lives with love and joy, the logical primary act is to shift our focus of attention to where these feelings originate.

However, for a great many of us, the emotional experience we all too often encounter when we turn our focus of attention to our hearts can be less than blissful. In fact very often we find our hearts feeling emotions we most definitely prefer to avoid – all the emotional and seemingly physical hurting, aching, suffering, all the agony of heartbreaks we have experienced in the past, and the contracted anxiety about having our heart hurt if we open up in the present moment. Who wants to focus on reliving all the pain and grief and rejection that we've felt (and continue to feel) in our hearts?

Unless you belong to the tiny percentage that defies the general statistics, growing up inevitably involves a fair amount of heartbreak and all its related negative feelings. Plus, childhood at best includes regular bouts of insecurity, bashfulness, apprehensions, not to mention confusions, disappointments, bouts of guilt, inadequacy, and the most devastating feeling of being abandoned, of being unloved and perhaps even unlovable. And as we move through puberty and into young adulthood, we all too often get lambasted with romantic disasters that make us feel like we can't even live through the heartbreaks that inevitably arise.

What did we all do, inside our own heads, to somehow protect ourselves from the overwhelming agonies of the heart that seem to define growing up and out into the world? Well, we armed ourselves from overmuch emotional stress by distancing ourselves as best we could from our own hearts – by retreating into our thinking minds, getting lost in safe fantasies, indulging in good old memories, or perhaps through immersing ourselves in physical activities such as sports, watching TV, reading books – any number of external stimuli that serve to keep our focus of attention away from painful and scary feelings in our hearts.

Now along comes some psychologist guy saying, hey, rather than running away from our heart feelings, let's start focusing much more regular and deep attention on the heart region, let's open up wide and once again feel what's happening in the heart!

Sure, fat chance of that. Why open up to old agonies?

Well, because it's also human nature to hunger for regular engagement with the vast array of positive feelings we're capable of experiencing in our hearts, if only we risk tuning into that deep-feeling realm of experience. Life without heart is, upon final analysis, total hell. Without heart we are shut off from love itself, because love is an experience of the heart. Without love we feel like there's an insidious, invisible emotional and spiritual membrane separating us from feeling the joy of life, from feeling loved by those around us, from feeling spontaneous, alive.

What's to be done? I have a compromise to suggest, based on what we've learned in this book. If you will risk regularly turning your focus of attention back toward the feelings you find in your heart, I'll offer a successful way to face the negative feelings you encounter there, so you can work through them to the point where, whenever you turn your attention to your heart, the good feelings will override the bad feelings – and you'll love to live in your heart again.

As I encourage you to look to your own heart experientially, let's also take essential time to look at the reality of how your various brains interact, to generate the experience of emotional feelings in your heart. As a first experiment, I'm going to have you pause in a moment and tune into the feelings (or seeming lack of feelings) and see if you can observe exactly how feelings are stimulated in your heart. Then we'll look at the psychological and neurological understanding of what you just experienced.

PAUSE AND EXPERIENCE
•

After reading this paragraph, close your eyes, tune into your breathing . . . and focus your mind's full attention on your heart, and the feelings you find there. Don't judge the feelings, just feel them . . . and as you stay aware of your breathing for perhaps a dozen full breaths, observe how your mind goes into action on various levels of thinking, remembering, imagining, and feeling . . . open up to your heart, and experience what comes . . .

How the Heart Feels Emotions

For some of you, I'm sure your experience in looking to your heart was like looking at a blank wall – nothing there. If so, don't despair. A great many of us are basically blocked altogether most of the time when we look to our hearts. We're playing it totally safe in life because we're afraid to be plunged once again into the overwhelming agony that our hearts can experience.

But rather than a blank, a lot of you found that there's a chronic aching in your heart, a combination of numbness and pain that doesn't feel good at all. Others of you quickly encountered a bunch of memories flooding your mind, about people who've hurt you by rejecting you one way or another. Some of you immediately found yourself thinking about, rather than being in, your heart. And many of you didn't encounter any present blocks, and were able to feel good in your heart today, without the past dragging you into remembering experiences that make you feel bad.

And here we find the key insight of this discussion, regarding the root source of all the bad feelings you encounter in your heart in the present moment. These feelings aren't being generated at all by anything happening in the present moment. They are not a product of perceptions, of participating in what's happening in the here and now. They are solely a product of memory.

You'll remember that neurologically the heart is connected strongly to the limbic part of your brain, to the mammalian brain that orchestrates your memories and the emotions associated with those memories. A major aspect of the heart dimension of our mind-brain seems to be its role in manifesting a present-moment experience based on memories we're running through our minds. We think of someone we love, we remember this person from past experiences, and these memories and thoughts in turn awaken in our heart region the physical experience of the emotion of caring. Thus the past can be brought alive in the present moment through our feelings in the heart.

This is a very important function of the heart-mind, and certainly in many cases very positive. It is how mammals bond with their family members, for instance, and how we bond with those who have given us pleasure rather than pain in the past. Our heart is the remarkable transformer that can create present-moment bodily feelings related to past experiences. We can also imagine something in the future happening with someone, and feel intense emotions in our hearts as well. In a sense, our hearts have the amazing power to break beyond linear time and space, and fill us full of loving feelings even when the object of our love is not here now.

Unfortunately, the opposite can also happen. We can remember negative experiences where a loving bond was broken, and get stuck remembering that negative experience, virtually for the rest of our lives. It's almost impossible, for instance, to go through puberty without falling wildly in love for the first time – and one way or another, having at some point to part with that first love, and suffer the agony of loss and heartbreak in the process. How many of us, after all, stay with our first wild love for the rest of our lives?

Hold in mind that we're talking about a function of the mammalian brain here, a familial-mate bonding process that in the wild works beautifully for most mammalian species. However, our human society has become so vastly complex that rather than the radical power of first love cementing into lifelong bonding, where hearts entrain romantically and never break that entrainment, we almost all get our hearts broken – and carry that primal wound throughout our lives.

I guarantee that all the pain in your heart is a product of memory, not a product of the present moment. And I guarantee that the pain in your heart is being kept alive, rather than let go of, because the experience that originally hurt you is being kept alive by the thoughts, attitudes, beliefs, and expectations that emerged out of the original experience.

In other words, we're back where we started. The thoughts that are chronically running through your mind, often at subliminal levels of recognition, are chronically stimulating particular emotions in your heart. Some of these emotions are joyful and some of them are agonizing and some are anywhere in between. But still, as long as your mind is running on automatic pilot based on past conditionings, your heart is going to be a victim of whatever memories and associations, beliefs and apprehensions, your mind happens to fixate upon at any given moment.

I'm here to blow the whistle on this victimization of your heart by your thinking and remembering (past-fixated) mind. Specifically, I'm here to point out that you have the choice of wallowing the rest of your life in past emotions, or shifting into a state of present-moment consciousness where your heart can perform its other primal emotional role in your life – that of responding directly in the present moment, to whatever you are perceiving in the present moment.

Letting Your Heart Speak

We've been exploring how your mind can function in several quite distinct ways. We're now at the point of final payoff where everything we've discussed in this book comes together to create a greater whole, because we're now ready to plug the heart-brain into the equation and see what happens when we quiet the thinking mind, shift from past-future into present-moment, and then open up to the experience we feel in our hearts, when we're managing our minds to our full advantage.

As long as we're locked in thinking mode, as long as we're busy processing past memories and beliefs and imaginations, we're stuck inside our own heads, virtually cut off from this one ever-present point in time where we can interact with the world around us, and thus learn new ways of being in the world. This entire book is focused on learning how to shift from thought fixation, to experience fixation. And when we plug the heart-brain into the equation, it all makes sense – the heart is a purely present-moment awareness, an emotion generator, if you will, that can be connected either to our limbic brain, which is past experience, or to our perceptual brain, which is present-moment experience.

When we have our focus on the past, on memories and thoughts emerging from those memories, our hearts are simply puppets generating whatever emotions are associated with our past experiences. No learning is taking place, no healing is taking place, when we're just replaying memories and emotions from the past. We're stuck with whatever our minds are choosing to dredge up at the moment.

However, we do have the freedom to manage our minds consciously and put a halt to all the replays and prepro-grammed emotions of past seasons of our lives. We have the power to shift to the present moment, quiet our usual associative murmurings about what's happened to us in the past – and tune into a function of the brain where the heart plays an entirely different, and truly exalted, role.

Let's say you meet someone new and are face-to-face with

this person in the present moment. This person is unique, and if you stay in the present moment with them and allow your perceptions and your heart feelings in the present moment to be dominant, you're going to have a unique encounter with this person, and develop a unique relationship based on the experiences that come to you in the present moment. Your heart is going to be able to respond directly to this person's heart as an experience, through all the sense inputs you're receiving of this person, and also through the more subtle communications where your minds and your hearts are interacting directly, as we saw earlier in this chapter.

In a word, you're going to interact. You're going to feel each other's presence directly, and meet, heart to heart. Something is going to happen between you, and this happening will continue to develop, moment to moment, as long as you remain focused on your present moment experience of each other, rather than on the memories that are already beginning to accumulate.

But what usually happens when we meet someone new? Almost instantly, our perceptions in the present moment stimulate associations with similar people in the past, and we begin to sink into judgmental thoughts and feelings about this person. We remember people similar to them and our judgments about these people. We remember emotions we felt for similar people, and our hearts get hit not with direct experience of this person in the present moment but with the emotions we felt with similar people in the past – we lose the real person before us and get lost in associative memories and feelings that might have nothing to do with this unique person at all.

I hope this vast difference in how we can manage our minds is now vibrantly clear. Of course, it's important to let our past

experiences speak and shed their impressions of how the present situation is somewhat similar to past experiences. But it's
vital that the past not dominate the present! Otherwise we
won't benefit from the wisdom of the heart in guiding us in
the present moment.

In the present moment, when we listen to what our hearts
are telling us about what we're experiencing, we gain direct
insight and wisdom into the deeper reality before us. When
our heart feel directly the harmonic or discordant feelings in
the other person's heart, we instantly "know" the truth about
this person's present inner condition – and we will respond to
this person accordingly. Leading thus with the feeling heart
rather than with the thinking mind is in no way foolish as
many people assume. Leading with the heart in our present-
moment encounters is the only wise way to approach life, because the heart as a present-moment sensing organ is our very
best system for directly knowing the truth about the situation.

Of course, when the heart speaks to us, this doesn't mean
that we've shut down the rest of the brain. It means just exactly
the opposite, that we've integrated the entire brain into one intuitive whole, where we can perceive the whole at once, and
act accordingly. This is how we can be thoughtless, and totally lucid. This is how we can move through the power of
love in the world and fear no harm – because love is not blind,
love is the permeating creative force of the universe itself. Love
is the heart of awareness, and awareness is our tool with which
we survive and thrive in the world.

Here's the optimum scenario as I see it: In any given moment, we first tune into how our heart is responding to the
reality of the situation. Once we've tuned into this primal
sense organ, and its response to all our sensory and energetic
inputs, we can allow this primal wisdom to influence our

thinking minds and interact with our memory-association banks . . . and almost instantly, we'll find ourselves thinking thoughts that are inspired by our hearts, and that therefore are truly wise and to be trusted.

That's the optimum dynamic for mind management with the heart as central, and the rest of the brain working in harmony with the heart. When we let our hearts speak, we are centered in love, and all shall unfold beautifully, spontaneously, and in harmony with the world around us.

Healing Old Heart Wounds

The basic rule of the heart seems to be this: Hold your awareness in the present moment as much as possible, so that the heart is able to be fully active in guiding and creating the unique experience happening right here, right now. However, very often old emotional wounds act like magnets in pulling our attention away from the present moment, toward emotional pain in the past. How can you heal and let go of old heart wounds, so that you're free to focus openly on what's happening here and now?

Heart Opening 1: Observation

If you find that old emotional pains dominate your heart feelings, you'll need to set aside time regularly for a few weeks to directly deal with these feelings, and let go of them. To begin the process, you will need to be brave enough to look toward your heart, and simply experience whatever happens when you do this. Spend five minutes or more at a time, pausing in a contemplative spirit to look to your heart, and experience the reality of your present condition.

The basic "quiet mind" process is the tool you will use, to

turn your attention toward your heart. Feel the air flowing in and out of your nose . . . expand your awareness to include the movements in your chest and belly as you breathe . . . expand your awareness to also include your heart, beating right in the middle of your breathing . . . and simply experience whatever happens . . . observe whatever feelings and memories and images come to mind . . . notice what thoughts begin to pass through your mind related to the emotions you find in your heart . . . observe directly and accept whatever you feel in your heart, today . . .

The key word here is *acceptance.* You will heal your old wounds by accepting them. These wounds exist in memory; they happened in the past. You cannot change what happened in the past. Therefore, you must accept the reality of what happened to you, rather than fighting and denying it. You must stop judging other people for what they did to you, because the past is nonnegotiable. It happened. Accept the reality of what happened – and you will become free of its power over you.

Heart Opening 2: Description

This acceptance can of course take time. Here's how to accelerate the acceptance process. Once you've spent time looking to your own heart's condition, get out a pen and paper and, after reflection, write down a description of the condition of your heart. Specifically, write down what emotions you find dominating your heart, what memories are dominating your mind, what thoughts about the memories are dominating your experience. Get to the source stimulant of your feelings, and write down this source. What is the thought behind the memory?

Also, write down who you think is responsible, who is to blame, for the emotional pain you're suffering. Take time to fully express yourself on paper, because this honest self-evaluation is vital to the further process coming next.

Heart Opening 3: Intent

Once you have fully described your heart feelings and condition, reflect upon what changes you would like to manifest in your life, related to your heart. In the case of a broken heart, for instance, you might want to state that you intend to recover from the heartbreak, let go of feeling hurt and vulnerable and hopeless and all the other feelings that you found . . . so you can heal and feel good again in your heart, and open yourself to love again more fully in the present moment. Be clear that you want to let go of the past – if indeed this is true.

Heart Opening 4: De-Beliefing

We now apply the basic formula we learned earlier for discovering and dealing with the underlying thoughts, beliefs, assumptions, and apprehensions that are chronically provoking aching painful emotional feelings in your heart. We've seen that whatever the memory-based emotions might be that you're feeling in your heart, they're being provoked by your own mental attitudes and self-judgments, by blaming other people for your own problems, and in general believing certain assumptions that make you feel terrible inside. To heal the heart, you'll need to let go of the beliefs that provoke the emotions that in turn are gripping your heart. Here's the basic process.

1. From the second step above, write down a statement about who is responsible, who is to blame.

2. Now ask yourself: Is this negative judgment really valid?

3. Now ask: How might I be benefiting from continuing to hold onto the thoughts and attitudes that make me suffer?

4. Now consider: What would happen if I let go of the belief that torments me?

Heart Opening 5: Healing

Once you've fully evaluated the assumptions and judgments, beliefs and memories, that generate the emotional contractions and pains in your heart, and seen the effects of these chronic thoughts, you can actively choose to stop judging, stop accusing – just accept the past, let go, and move on.

Often it is very helpful to state to yourself or out loud, the step or steps you are now ready to make (assuming you are ready, of course) in order to move out of past feelings, and open up to present-moment encounters of the heart.

What is it you need to say, to free yourself? Perhaps the first statement is, "I forgive Ginny – it's not her fault I'm hurting." Maybe this statement is enough to live with, for a few days. Then return to this step, and see what you need to state next, to let go of your past pain. Perhaps it's, "I'm not hopeless – I can take care of myself," or "I know I'm lovable, because I love and accept myself just as I am," or similar expressions that begin to lighten your own self-judgment so that you can indeed love again.

And the primary statement, of course, that you want to say over and over again from your depths, is, "I'm ready to let go of the heartbreak, I'm ready to heal emotionally, and feel better in my heart. I'm ready to open up and love again."

Heart Opening 6: Opening

Such a recovery process takes time of course. The heart can

be so contracted that months must be devoted to helping it recover. But it's essential to take this time, because life simply isn't worth living when the heart is shut down in pain. Healing must take place. Often it does naturally, of course, over time. But conscious techniques for letting go and moving on can speed up and ensure the process.

And once your heart begins feeling better, lighter, more ready to risk again, it's important first to purposefully nurture your own love for yourself, as we've seen earlier. The true healing of the heart happens when you stop judging yourself deep down, and accept yourself with unconditional love.

Once you establish this foundation of self-love, you won't be so vulnerable to having your heart broken by other people, because you won't be depending on them for that ultimate feeling of being loved – you'll be giving that to yourself regularly. As soon as you mature to where you look to yourself, rather than to a mother or father figure, for your primary feeling of being loved, you'll be able to spread love freely without becoming dependent on the people you love for a level of support that only you can give yourself.

Living in Your Heart

Now that we've seen the therapeutic healing process for learning to feel good when you look to your heart, we can present the shorter route that will work for many of you. This involves simply turning your attention to your heart in the present moment, and at the same time, using your own thoughts to point your attention toward good feelings already living inside your heart. This is a type of positive conditioning that will throw the balance away from pain toward love, within your own heart experience.

Obviously, along with the hurting experiences you've encountered heart-wise, you've also had a multitude of good, warm, and loving experiences. All too often, because of a negative self-image, people get fixated on the pain and ignore the pleasure – because of the beliefs they're holding onto. For instance, many people carry the unspoken belief that "I've had a terrible love life," or "Nobody seems to love me," or "Life's basically a painful experience," or "Love never works out anyway," and because these beliefs dominate the mind, one's inner voice tends to think about and recall all the negative memories that support the belief.

This is the basic dynamic of the mind, as we've seen – that the thoughts and memories and images that flow chronically through our minds are mostly determined by our underlying assumptions about life and about ourselves. If we think nobody loves us, we tend not to remember the many times when someone has loved us. We live in a self-fulfilling prophesy of the experiences we allow to come to us.

I am here to encourage you to do just the opposite. Regardless of your present heart condition, regardless of all the bad things that have happened to you that can hold your heart contracted and closed down, begin using wisely and to your advantage that one power you have at your disposal every moment of your day – your power of attention.

Specifically, begin focusing on good feelings that you have experienced in your heart, when you were in a loving mood, and feeling well-loved. It doesn't matter if it was the Queen of Sheba who was being accepting and loving to you, or the neighbor's dog, or the postman or cashier or whoever. What's important is regularly focusing your attention, as a new habit, on memories that support your capacity to love and be loved.

Regularly nurture yourself with positive memories when your heart felt good and your spirit was expansive, so that you decondition the belief that all you've felt in the past was a lack of love in your life.

And of course, regularly take the time to develop the primary habit of shifting out of the past altogether, and tuning into whatever good feelings you find in the present moment. The most powerful reconditioning force is always the experience coming to you in the present moment, where you put aside all expectations and encounter reality as it emerges in your senses, here and now. The following primary guided experience will help you over the next days and weeks and months and years to go more and more deeply into the wisdom and love always alive and ready to manifest, from the very center of your silent heart.

We've covered a great amount in this chapter concerning the vast depths to be discovered in your heart, when you learn to quiet the thinking mind and listen to what your heart's wisdom has to say each and every day. Let's now end the discussion with a guided experience that will bring you regularly in touch with your own heart, help heal old wounds that cause heartache, and encourage an ever-expanding sense of love both toward yourself and toward those around you.

This special session is designed to be experienced perhaps once a week, for the rest of your life. Why? Because we are continually in the process of dealing with old emotional wounds that have been rejected and buried earlier in our lives (usually from childhood), and are now finally rising to the surface to be accepted, experienced, and let go of. I've been doing this basic process for thirty years now, and always look forward to seeing if there's any emotional pressure inside me this week that begs for attention, love, and release.

This is how we stay healthy emotionally – through regularly looking, accepting, releasing, and healing whatever emotional pressure we might find within us. However, the heart story doesn't end with the healing of old emotional wounds. It's vital in each and every heart-healing session to first open up and deal with whatever heart wounds desire attention, and then to move on to a purely enjoyable heart-awakening process in the present moment, where we affirm our love for ourselves and those around us, open our hearts to deep entrainment with the greater love of the universe and beyond, and learn more and more to dwell within our hearts as our center of being.

I suggest that you read through the following script of the guided session, just to get a feel for where it takes you. Then either memorize the process so you can do it on your own, or have a friend guide you through it, or go online and let me guide you through the process via streamed audio. (www.john selby.com)

GUIDED SESSION 4:
SILENCE AND YOUR HEART
•

First of all, as usual, make sure you're comfortable, perhaps lying on your back if that's best today . . . take a few enjoyable breaths to just relax . . . stretch if you want to . . . yawn perhaps . . . let your breaths come and go without any effort . . . let your breathing stop when it wants to . . . and start when it wants to . . .

And begin to notice the air flowing in and out your nose or mouth as you breathe . . . just tune into the sensations coming to you, in your nose . . . your chest and belly . . . be aware of your feet . . . your hands . . . your head . . . your skin covering your whole body . . . listen to the sounds around you . . .

Let your awareness gently turn toward your heart, beating right in the middle of your breathing . . . just accept whatever feelings or lack of feelings you find in your heart right now . . . breathe through your mouth if you find any emotional pressure . . . let your feelings be there . . . accept them . . . love them, whatever they are . . . and let them flow . . .

Notice if you have any emotions inside you, aimed at a particular person . . . remember the memories associated with this person . . . relive whatever experiences come to mind . . . and now imagine that person is before you right now . . . go ahead and say what you want to say to them to express your emotions toward them . . . don't hold back, be honest . . . get it off your chest . . .

Now let them talk to you, about how they feel about you and your feelings . . . let them say what they have to say, listen without judging them . . . take them in . . . now you can talk to them again, really say what's on your heart . . . open up and get it all out . . . and if you can, begin to accept what happened to you in the past . . . forgive whatever happened . . . accept the past . . . and let it go . . .

And when you're finished, just relax . . . stay with your feelings as they calm down . . . let your face muscles relax . . . your jaw relax . . . your tongue relax . . . and your emotions relax inside your heart . . . tune into the sounds around you . . . the sensations of your breaths coming . . . and going . . .

And bring your focus of attention gently to your heart . . . right in the middle of your breathing . . . and see how you feel in your heart when you say to yourself a few times, "I accept myself, just as I am . . ."

And now say to yourself a few times, and see how it feels in your heart, "I open my heart, and love myself . . ."

Breathe . . . make no effort . . . just be here . . . your mind quiet . . . your emotions quiet . . . your heart open . . . to love . . . let your heart heal . . . let the love flow in . . . let your heart feel good inside your chest right now . . .

And when you're ready, you can begin to stretch a little . . . yawn perhaps . . . and at your own leisure, finish this session with your heart open to yourself and those around you . . . and go on about your day spreading acceptance . . . trust . . . and love . . .

For streamed-audio guidance through this experience, go to www.johnselby.com.

part two

life applications

chapter 5

not lonely when alone

———————

We've now completed the intensive chapters of this book, and can relax into shorter, less demanding discussions as we explore how to apply what we've learned, to specific situations where a purposefully quiet mind can prove to be an ultimate blessing.

In this chapter we'll consider how to thrive when alone instead of getting stuck in loneliness or indulging in chronic thoughts that drag us down. In Chapter 6 we'll clarify how to apply our quiet-mind procedures to the workplace to optimize both success and enjoyment on the job. Chapter 7 will elucidate one of the primal ways in which quieting the mind can transform our lives – in this case, our sexual experience. And in Chapter 8 we'll discuss the close of the day and our ability to manage our minds just before bedtime so as to encourage a good night's sleep filled with much-needed rest and dreams that serve us rather than disturb us.

We tend to have two personalities – who we are as social beings, and who we are as solitary beings. When we're with another person or in a group, we tend to be engaged in vocal intercourse where, rather than just thinking inside our own minds without our bodies much engaged, we relate with our whole bodies using both our physical movements and our vocalization system to interact with those around us.

There's a vast difference between thinking and talking. When we talk with someone, our thoughts emerge from a somewhat different source than when we're alone thinking about something. Talking is very much a present-moment experience in which we're aware of our bodily stance, our hand movements, and especially our tongues and lungs as we push air out and vibrate our vocal cords in order to create meaningful sounds to communicate our inner ideas and feelings.

Therefore our thinking tends to be more spontaneous when we're talking. In fact, we often surprise ourselves by what we say – we become inspired in the act of speaking, tapping a wellspring of wisdom and integrated understanding that emerges within the expansive realms of the present-moment act of speaking. We also tend to be more aware of our hearts, so we're in touch with our deeper feelings as we communicate our ideas to the outside world. We'll look at this social aspect of thinking in Chapters 6 and 7.

We do most of our thinking, however, not when talking, but when in solitary mode. Whether we're left alone for just a few moments, or find ourselves alone for days on end, the solitary experience lends itself to a withdrawal into our thinking minds and a loss of whole-body present-moment consciousness.

How we manage our minds when alone determines a great deal of how we thrive or suffer in life. I'd like to provide you with a concrete format through which you can begin to evaluate your solitary habits of mind, and modify or transform these habits if you find that they don't serve you well.

Your Solitary Behavior Patterns

The key to successful mind management when you are alone is simple observation of your present habits of mind. What do you actually do when you are alone?

Here's a fairly long list of things that you might do and emotions you might feel when you're alone. I recommend going through this list thoughtfully and honestly once a week for a month or two and observe how your solitary habits are changing or staying the same. This reflective process will also make yourself more conscious of how you are choosing to spend each moment of your solitary time. Hold in mind that solitary time also includes every moment when you are with someone but not relating with them.

WHAT I DO WHEN I'M ALONE

1. When I'm alone, I watch television . . .
   ❑ a lot   ❑ often   ❑ sometimes   ❑ not much   ❑ almost never

2. When I'm alone, I read . . .
   ❑ a lot   ❑ often   ❑ sometimes   ❑ not much   ❑ almost never

3. When I'm alone, I drink alcohol and/or take various other drugs . . .
   ❑ a lot   ❑ often   ❑ sometimes   ❑ not much   ❑ almost never

4. When I'm alone, I exercise . . .
   ❑ a lot   ❑ often   ❑ sometimes   ❑ not much   ❑ almost never

5. When I'm alone, I eat . . .
   ❑ a lot   ❑ often   ❑ sometimes   ❑ not much   ❑ almost never

6. When I'm alone, I go out for walks or ride a bike . . .
   ❏ a lot   ❏ often   ❏ sometimes   ❏ not much   ❏ almost never

7. When I'm alone, I laze around or sleep . . .
   ❏ a lot   ❏ often   ❏ sometimes   ❏ not much   ❏ almost never

8. When I'm alone, I sit at the computer . . .
   ❏ a lot   ❏ often   ❏ sometimes   ❏ not much   ❏ almost never

9. When I'm alone, I get creative and do fun projects . . .
   ❏ a lot   ❏ often   ❏ sometimes   ❏ not much   ❏ almost never

WHAT I DO INSIDE MY OWN MIND

10. When I'm alone, I sit around and think . . .
    ❏ a lot   ❏ often   ❏ sometimes   ❏ not much   ❏ almost never

11. When I'm alone, I worry about things . . .
    ❏ a lot   ❏ often   ❏ sometimes   ❏ not much   ❏ almost never

12. When I'm alone, I dream of the future . . .
    ❏ a lot   ❏ often   ❏ sometimes   ❏ not much   ❏ almost never

13. When I'm alone, I imagine erotic situations and excite myself
    sexually . . .
    ❏ a lot   ❏ often   ❏ sometimes   ❏ not much   ❏ almost never

14. When I'm alone, I drop into the same old boring habits . . .
    ❏ a lot   ❏ often   ❏ sometimes   ❏ not much   ❏ almost never

15. When I'm alone, I remember the past . . .
    ❏ a lot   ❏ often   ❏ sometimes   ❏ not much   ❏ almost never

16. When I'm alone, I tune into the present moment . . .
    ❏ a lot   ❏ often   ❏ sometimes   ❏ not much   ❏ almost never

17. When I'm alone, I sit and meditate or contemplate . . .
    ❏ a lot   ❏ often   ❏ sometimes   ❏ not much   ❏ almost never

HOW I FEEL WHEN I'M ALONE

18. When I'm alone, I feel content and happy . . .
    ❑ a lot   ❑ often   ❑ sometimes   ❑ not much   ❑ almost never

19. When I'm alone, I feel lonely and sad . . .
    ❑ a lot   ❑ often   ❑ sometimes   ❑ not much   ❑ almost never

20. When I'm alone, I get agitated and frustrated . . .
    ❑ a lot   ❑ often   ❑ sometimes   ❑ not much   ❑ almost never

21. When I'm alone, I think about the people I miss . . .
    ❑ a lot   ❑ often   ❑ sometimes   ❑ not much   ❑ almost never

22. When I'm alone, I just do what comes spontaneously . . .
    ❑ a lot   ❑ often   ❑ sometimes   ❑ not much   ❑ almost never

23. When I'm alone, I sit around and feel bored with life . . .
    ❑ a lot   ❑ often   ❑ sometimes   ❑ not much   ❑ almost never

24. When I'm alone, I feel depressed . . .
    ❑ a lot   ❑ often   ❑ sometimes   ❑ not much   ❑ almost never

25. When I'm alone, I feel blissful and radiantly happy . . .
    ❑ a lot   ❑ often   ❑ sometimes   ❑ not much   ❑ almost never

---

PAUSE AND EXPERIENCE
•

You might want to pause right now, and go back to consider this list of solitary choices more carefully. For each statement, be sure to tune into your breathing . . . your heart . . . your whole-body presence . . . and in this relaxed open state of consciousness, consider each statement and see what reflections and insights spontaneously come to mind right now, as you hold your mind's focus of attention on the statement and all that it implies . . .

Always Your Choice

Based on how you responded to these solitary-habits statements and how you feel about the behavior patterns this list
brought to the light, you can begin to run your mind and behavior more to your liking by remembering that you do have
the freedom to choose where to focus your attention, every
moment of your solitary life. You're being run either by past
conditioning and beliefs about how you should behave, or by
present-moment decisions and choices that you make with
your whole being in the here and now.

Some time ago, while living my own quite solitary life in retreat down in Guatemala, I wrote a small book called *Solitude: The Art of Living with Yourself,* and indeed it is an art,
to create each new emerging moment so that it has beauty,
grace, purpose, clarity, and meaning. Your entire life can be
seen as a work of art in action, if only you approach your own
beingness in this creative light. And at the center of this art-
work is your creation of a unique ever-expanding relationship
with your own self.

As I said in *Solitude,* "The essential challenge in all our lives
is to master the fine art of developing a healthy, fulfilling relationship with ourselves. It is tragic that with all the educa-
tion we receive as children, we are very seldom taught the
basic skills for developing a deep intimate relationship with
ourselves. Instead, most of us grow up conditioned to fear
solitude, and develop the habit of avoiding encounters with
our inner spirit."

Why do so many of us fear solitude, and do everything we
can to avoid being alone with ourselves without constant distraction? Because with our prevailing negative attitudes about
our own selves, we're afraid to come face-to-face with aspects

of our own selves that we reject, that we're afraid of, that we fear will make us suffer or react with self-loathing.

If you find that, indeed, you tend to avoid encounters with your own inner spirit, it's certainly time to look into this reactionary habit, and learn to enjoy every moment of solitude that comes to you, as an opportunity to hang out with yourself – with your best friend on Earth! The earlier chapters have given you the tools you will need to change your beliefs about yourself if you find them negative. And there's no better way to find out about your own beliefs than when you're alone, with unstructured time, and able to observe how you relate to your own self when there's no distraction to save you from this face-to-face encounter.

Your Own Best Friend?

Again, a series of short focusing questions can work wonders in helping you to clarify how you feel about yourself, and therefore how you approach being alone with yourself.

1. Do you like yourself?
2. Do you enjoy spending time alone with yourself?
3. Do you feel good in your heart, toward yourself?
4. Do you look forward to time alone?
5. Do you accept yourself just as you are?
6. Do you consider yourself a beautiful person deep down?
7. Are you in love with yourself?
8. Is there passion in your relationship with your own self?
9. Do you like the feeling of living inside your own skin?
10. When you're alone, are you content to just "be" with yourself?
11. Would you like to feel better toward yourself?
12. What would happen if you accepted yourself, just as you are?

PAUSE AND EXPERIENCE

•

Pause, go ahead and read each of these questions again, remembering to stay aware of your breathing . . . your heart . . . your whole-body presence . . . and allow insights to come spontaneously to mind as you reflect upon each question . . .

Escaping Loneliness

All of us seem to have bouts of loneliness, regardless of whether we're living alone or with other people. One of the most curious observations of therapists and counselors is that so many people report feeling lonely a great deal of the time, even when they seem to be well-loved. How can we suffer from loneliness, even to the point of depression and despair, when we're surrounded by people who care for us?

The answer is obvious yet all too often overlooked. If we don't have a successful relationship with our own selves, if we're rejecting and judging and pushing away inside our own skins, we're going to feel the utter inner agony of being hopelessly distanced from the one person in the world that we yearn radically to feel close to – our own selves.

So what do we do? Very often, we run away from the vacancy inside our own hearts, and try to immerse ourselves in social situations and relationships so that we feel loved, even if we don't love ourselves. This is a primary escape route for people who are lonely – they keep themselves constantly active at work, in social and church groups, in sports and family affairs. But still, they never quite get away from their sense of isolation from their own souls. They run as far as they can from the inherent loneliness of not accepting themselves – but there's just nowhere they can run to be free from the emptiness inside their own hearts.

A great many people also try to escape their loneliness by becoming supergivers to the rest of the world. They are continually giving caring attention to those around them. They exert great effort to serve humankind, to seek and find love wherever they can. Many people also run from one love affair to the next, determined that they will someday find someone who will miraculously through the power of love, heal their hearts, make them feel whole inside, and take away the chronic ache of loneliness from their lives.

It never works. When we don't love ourselves, and accept ourselves, and be best friends with ourselves, when we hold thoughts and attitudes and judgments and beliefs about our own selves that are negative, we make ourselves unlovable – and therefore unable to establish relationships that are fulfilling.

Look at it this way. If we don't like ourselves, how will anyone else be able to like us? If we haven't nurtured our own inner realms to where love is alive and flourishing inside our hearts for our own selves, there will be nothing really to us that another person can love. We've made ourselves basically unlovable, and then we complain about being lonely and no one loving us.

If we want to enjoy solitude, if we want to be able to be alone without feeling lonely, if we want to move beyond loneliness into fulfilling relationships, we simply must first of all nurture our own love for ourselves. And this is not accomplished in social settings, it is accomplished most effectively by spending time alone with ourselves, working through all the negative self-judgments we picked up in the past, letting go of them and opening our hearts to ourselves.

How can you best approach the essential task of nurturing

your relationship with your own self? Chapter 2 covered the basic process for identifying the thoughts that are disabling your ability to love yourself without judgment. This chapter can further aid you in learning to love yourself more fully by shedding light on how solitude can be your best friend in helping you move through the process that leads to self-love.

Specifically, let's identify how and where personal growth takes place, so that you can begin to choose to spend more time focusing on this issue. Clearly, personal growth requires the time and space to reflect, to observe, to interact with your own behavioral and cognitive habits so that they can begin to evolve in directions you prefer. This is why being alone is essential to personal growth – and why people who avoid being alone with themselves tend to appear shallow and caught in emotional and mental ruts that don't serve them. We do have to retreat regularly and devote time to our relationship with our selves if that relationship is to flourish – that's obvious. Thus the primal need for time alone . . .

Now let's consider what your options are when you're alone. Of the list of things you might do when alone, which ones will offer you time and space to develop and improve your relationship with yourself? Let's look at them one by one.

When you're *watching television,* is this an activity that lends itself to self-reflection, or is it a way of avoiding coming face-to-face with yourself and working things out? In most cases, watching television tends to be an avoidance pattern, rather than a nurturing pattern – so each time you sit down to lose yourself in TV, consider that you can choose to do something more nurturing to your self-relationship.

When you're *reading,* is this an escape from yourself or are you nurturing your friendship with yourself? It can be either, depending on the book and the way in which you read the book. Some books – hopefully, this one, for instance – are designed to give you space to reflect, to grow. So you have the choice of reading to escape yourself or to encounter yourself. Each time you sit down to read, reflect upon the choice you are making.

When you *exercise,* is this growth time or avoidance time? In my experience, getting the body moving, the heart pumping, moving the body in general, is a nurturing experience – especially because such exercise tends to be a whole-body present-moment pastime that awakens the deeper soul and integrates heart, mind, and body. However, many people put themselves in a trance of self-avoidance with exercise, in which they avoid their underlying emotions through extreme physical exertion. It's always important to regularly ask: What emotions are buried inside me? Am I using my exercise to run away from my own feelings toward myself?

What about *eating?* Certainly we need to eat, and the ritual of eating and satisfying a basic appetite can be fulfilling. However, all too often overeaters are trying to fulfill one hunger (self-love) with another (food). There is a craving not backed up by actual need – and this can be a prime time to sit down, look inward to the hunger, and see what assumptions and beliefs are attached to the thought, "I need to eat something to feel good." True or false? And what do you really need – what are you really hungering for?

Going outside for walks or bike rides when alone is often a very rewarding experience, because the movement tends to stop chronic thoughts and in-house activities and awaken present-moment consciousness and reflections. I personally don't know what I'd do without at least a half-hour brisk walk every day, because the state of consciousness I move into while walking through nature is uniquely nurturing, and the insights that come into my mind after a period of thoughtless walking are invaluable. Furthermore, getting out and walking is one of the primal activities of human beings, and to do this regularly takes us back into a sense of who we really are.

What about *just being lazy,* doing nothing, or drifting into sleep when alone? Although doing nothing can obviously be an avoidance habit when overindulged, there's a lot to be said for short regular episodes of being lazy and doing nothing, and I highly recommend at least half an hour of total laziness and goofing off every day. When we were very young, we did a lot of lazing around, of just goofing off with no intent, no future projection, just pure present-moment beingness. To simply "be" in the present moment with no thoughts of the future or the past – this is one of the nicest gifts we can give ourselves if we want to be best friends with ourselves. Also, giving ourselves permission to just let go once or twice a day to drift into a short sleep is immensely rejuvenating – and amazing insights often pop into mind.

Spending free time at the computer – does this really benefit us? My colleagues and I have been trying to devise online experiences that will nurture the soul; there's no reason why the computer can't be used for personal growth and valuable experience. We're entering a period of history when we can indeed be alone and receive considerable valuable guidance of the experiential kind from computer inputs. What's important is observing what state of consciousness we're entering into as we sit at the computer. If you're just passing time and avoiding yourself by staring at the computer screen, turn the thing off. If you're being guided in directions that lead to actual inner experience of value, then wonderful – technology is serving the spirit as it should.

What about *times of reflection?* Of course, a great deal of

time alone is spent in rumination, thinking about our lives, trying to come up with a better game plan for what we're going
to do next, trying to make sense out of how we're running
our lives. A certain amount of thinking is surely helpful, as
we seek to clarify with concepts the reality of our experience.
When thinking is performing its designated task of digesting
experience into meaningful concepts and game plans, this is
great. However, most thinking, because it is mostly focused on
the past or the future, tends to distance us from our feelings
and the experience of feeling good in our hearts toward ourselves in the present moment. Whenever you catch yourself
thinking, be sure to observe the content of your thoughts,
and regularly quiet all thoughts so as to shift into more heart-
centered modes of being.

Worrying when alone is perhaps the most common lonely
practice, and it serves almost no positive end. If this is an issue
for you (as it is for almost everyone), Chapter 3 offers techniques that are helpful in quieting worrisome mental habits.
The problem of worrying when alone is that we can get seriously lost in our anxious fantasies, often for hours on end, resulting in a general terrible feeling in the body and heart and
confusion in the mind. When you're alone, keep a lookout
for when you sink into worries – and deliberately choose to
quiet those worries or actively deal with them so that your
time alone isn't spent frozen in anxious feelings and thoughts.

And *future-tripping?* All of us, when we're alone with free
time, have the tendency to dream about how our future might
unfold. In itself, there's nothing wrong with this activity, and
unless we're imagining terrible things happening to us, we can
make ourselves feel quite good with our imaginings. We may
also develop some concrete ideas that will, hopefully, advance
from intent to actuality. The danger of daydreaming, even

though it can nurture our self-image and make us feel good inside, is that we're once again avoiding how we really feel right now in our hearts. Future-tripping all the time will not take away the loneliness. Always, it's important to spend regular time in the present moment dealing with whatever we find here, rather than being lost overmuch in the future.

The same goes for *remembering the past*. A certain amount of reflection upon past experiences is not only good but essential. We do need to integrate what happens to us, into an ever-expanding concept of what's going on in our lives. However, regularly getting lost in memories, even if this makes us feel happy and content by remembering good times in the past, won't lead to personal growth in the present moment. If you find that you indulge in the past too much, it's time to manage your mind and focus in directions that you know will directly encourage insight, healing, and awakening in the present moment. And if you find that you often get stuck remembering bad things that happened to you, definitely put an end to it. You're actually torturing yourself – and that's no way to treat your best friend.

If you find that you enjoy *tuning into the present moment* a lot when you're alone, relaxing and staying conscious of what's happening around you and within you moment by moment, and enjoying the pure pleasure of the sensations of being alive, great! You're optimizing your opportunity for loving yourself just as you are for getting to know yourself just "being" rather than engaged in "doing." By nurturing the open state of free play in the present moment, you make contact with your deeper self, whom you've known since you were very young, and you nurture that inner child who actually knows how to be your best friend at the deepest levels.

Spending time *meditating or contemplating* when you're alone,

if done in the spirit of present-moment awareness and engagement rather than as a trance-inducing process, is an optimum
way to nurture your self-acceptance and self-understanding.
Meditation at its core is simply tuning in to the present moment and allowing consciousness to expand in the present
moment, infinitely. In the process you tap into your ultimate
higher self. This is where the primal love comes flowing in to
your heart, allowing your sense of belonging to a greater whole
to emerge to entirely obliterate any feelings of loneliness.

If you regularly find that you feel *content and happy* when
alone, your thoughts quiet and your mind at peace, give this
book to a friend – you don't need it any longer. However, if
you often feel sad whenever you're alone, it's time to get to
work seriously with earlier chapters and programs in this book,
so you can discover what thoughts are habitually running
through your mind that generate the emotion of sadness in
your heart. Don't think that it's your fate to feel badly in your
heart. Act until your heart is singing again!

Agitation and frustration are very common conditions that
torture people when they're alone. There's the feeling of not
being able to sit still, of being driven constantly and never
finding any inner peace. There's the sensation of needing something, and being frustrated because you don't know what it
is or how to get it. Again, time to go to work, because these
emotions are strong indicators that there are beliefs inside
your own head that are driving you mad. Almost certainly
the agitation is being caused because you hunger for love and
self-acceptance, but are afraid to go through the process to
get what you hunger for. So you tend to be angry with yourself even more than before, and a vicious circle continues. The
only successful way of dealing with frustration and agitation
is to look directly inward, observe what's causing the feeling,

and question the beliefs and attitudes that you find. Go after them, question them, and put them aside if they are causing you pain, as you learned in Chapters 2 and 3.

If you find yourself often *thinking about people you miss* in your life, be careful you aren't overindulging in the past, which is gone, to the exclusion of the present, where you can establish relationships that will truly nurture you now – including your relationship with your own self. If you yearn for the old days, chances are, you felt good about yourself in the old days. It's time to feel that way again – not by reactivating memory banks of a long-lost past, but by opening your heart in the present moment, letting it heal and love again. As you saw, Chapter 4 is the key to that heart-awakening process.

Ah, then there's *boredom*. Most people who don't enjoy being alone are people locked into old habits of attention-focusing that they find boring. They think that life is boring – but the truth is, the only boring thing about life is their chronic avoidance of it! If you find yourself bored when alone, all you have to do is shift your focus of attention to the present moment and spontaneously respond to whatever happens next, inside or outside. Boredom is caused especially by rigid beliefs about what you should and should not do. When you set yourself free by entering the present moment and quieting your judgmental mind, the entire universe opens up to you. Your creativity comes into play – because you're shifting into play mode. Little kids don't get bored. Why? They live in the present moment. We can too. If we just listen to our hearts and set ourselves free to do what we want to, life emerges, creative projects come into being, and our hearts start singing again.

Okay, time for *the erotic side of life,* and the fact that we have the power to make ourselves feel good physically and

sexually. We've all been conditioned to think that making ourselves feel good in public is bad, and perhaps such inhibitions
are fine in society. However, when we're alone, should there be
any shoulds that limit our desire to make ourselves feel good?
A great many people masturbate when alone, and then feel
reflexively guilty or bad for having done so. Beliefs are the
source of the bad feelings. Are these beliefs valid? Question
them, and toss them out if they don't serve you. On the other
hand, masturbation of any kind can be an avoidance of other
feelings. The hunger to make love with another person, to
share the natural process of erogenous pleasure and ultimate
orgiastic release, is a natural hunger that makes us want to
leave our solitude – and that's great. Hold in mind, however,
that to share love we must love ourselves first, and in order
for someone to love us, we must first nurture love in our own
hearts.

Drinking alcohol has long been a primary way of avoiding
oneself when alone – a few drinks and you're transported beyond the thoughts and emotions that bother you when you're
alone and getting bit by loneliness. I'm not saying that drinking alcohol is nothing but an escape, nor even that such an escape isn't valid and enjoyable. However, it's important to
observe how you use alcohol if you use it regularly when you're
alone. Would you do better to face your demons and be rid
of them? Same with marijuana. As Dr. Francis Cheek at
NIMH demonstrated some time ago, this is a drug that directly shuts down many of the everyday types of reflection
and self-analysis, and feelings as well, that lead to emotional
growth. If you smoke as a habit when you're alone, you're seriously blocking your ability to move beyond emotions that
bother you. A few tokes now and then for inspiration and a
shift of perspective seem to do no harm, and often some good.

Regular use of any drug that enables you to avoid yourself will do just that – distance you from your self.

Almost everyone has bouts of *depression*. And depression shows up most often when we are alone with no social distraction. Depression is always a strong indicator that something in our inner being is being blocked. We saw earlier that the general de-beliefing process of cognitive therapy works well for reducing depression; even without a spiritual dimension such inner mind work, it is more effective in treating depression than any medication, and once the inner work is done the depression tends not to return.

You'll find this is true if you work with the programs presented earlier in this book. When you face your negative beliefs and assumptions that are dragging you down, you truly liberate yourself. If you find that you get depressed often when you're alone, it's time to actively confront the underlying chronic thoughts that are causing your depression – and move into the peace and joy of an accepting, quiet mind. If the programs in this book and online audio guidance do the trick, great. If not, I urge you to seek direct cognitive/spiritual therapy so you can successfully deal with your depression and can agree with the last statement on our list: "When I'm alone, I feel blissful and radiantly happy."

Alone but Not Lonely

Based on what we've learned thus far, let's look directly at the emotion of loneliness and, if loneliness is an issue in your life, discover how to most effectively reduce its grip on your life. I don't mean to give the impression that loneliness is a facile condition that can be wiped out of your experience with a few quick tricks. However, great strides can be made within just a few weeks, if you dedicate yourself to action rather than the usual passivity of the lonely-hearted. I'm going to cover a lot of ground in the next few paragraphs.

Feeling lonely after the loss of a loved one, and then wanting to find someone who will love us and take away our lonely feelings, is a natural human emotion. We are, after all, social as well as solitary beings, and it's a natural hunger to desire companionship, sexual intimacy, and feelings of belonging to a family or group. Loneliness becomes a problem when it becomes a chronic dominant emotion in our lives, beyond the usual time to recover from a broken heart or loss of a loved one. When loneliness takes us over and leaves us depressed and weak and unable to reach out to find new friends who satisfy our social and intimate needs, then it's time to do something specific with the cause of our lonely feelings.

As you might imagine by now, my understanding of chronic loneliness is that it's an emotion being regularly stimulated by habitual thought-flows running through your mind, which in turn are being generated by underlying negative attitudes about yourself and the world, which in turn are provoked by core beliefs or assumptions you learned early in life, and that need to be unearthed and revised to your advantage.

This is the conclusion thousands of therapists have reached after working with people suffering from chronic loneliness and seeing how it can be cured through cognitive therapy techniques and the attainment of a mind that has ceased thinking the following thought: "I'm not lovable . . . nobody likes me . . . it's hopeless . . . I've been abandoned."

Earlier, we talked about hardwired fears rooted in the amygdala and the limbic region of the brain. Fear of abandonment is one of those hardwired gut fears that can grip any of us when we perceive that we might be left out of the tribal circle.

The fear of being abandoned is obviously an infantile fear of
great survival value. It makes us cry out loudly whenever we
fear being left behind. In early human society, being left behind was almost certain death. To be excluded from the tribal
circle and refused participation in the group was tantamount
to death. No one could live alone and survive in primitive
times.

Therefore we fear being left alone. We fear losing the love
of our mother especially, because we are in her care for our
first years of life, and if she abandons us, we die. Because of this
hardwired reaction of fear related to abandonment, our early
relationship with our own mother is obviously crucial to our
underlying sense of well-being in later life. I'm not one to
point fingers at mothers for causing the emotional problems
of their children. However, we must face the fact that if we
didn't feel secure with our mother, if a certain trust was miss-
ing for whatever reason in our first few years of life, we're
going to carry with us at the amygdala level of consciousness
a certain fear of being abandoned.

Even if our mother loved us intensely and we never feared
abandonment, when we grow up and fall in love with someone and experience similar emotions of total trust and intimacy with our mate, if we then lose our bond with this person
for whatever reason, we're going to feel abandoned. This is
why heartbreak is such an intense experience – it pushes primal fear buttons.

Ten thousand years ago, if your mother left you when you
were very young, you would just lie there helplessly, until
some animal came along and ate you. Talk about feeling hopeless and unloved – this is the origin of that emotion. So whenever you feel in any way distanced from your primary mate
or family members or friends or social group, you're liable to

feel reaction from your amygdala and limbic system that ranges from loneliness to depression to abandonment.

The good news is that once you understand what's going on inside you, you can begin to catch your underlying attitudes and beliefs, question them, and break free of their grip. If you're feeling acute heartbreak or grief, you can begin to identify the thoughts and images dominating your mind right under the surface. If you have the courage to look right in the face of your loneliness, you'll find yourself caught up with thoughts such as, "I can't make it alone," or "I can't live without him (or her)," or "It's hopeless, I can't survive alone." Mixed with these thoughts, you'll almost certainly find thoughts such as, "Nobody loves me," "I'm no good," and so forth.

The result of being immersed in all these semiconscious thoughts will be as expected. Your heart, and by extension your whole body, will feel pathos, weakness, hopelessness, acute fear, and emotional pain, even the chronic anticipation of sudden attack and violent extinction. Grief and heartbreak are no fun. We possess a natural grieving process that heals our sense of loss when we don't have underlying negative attitudes about ourselves from early conditioning. But when we carry early programmings about abandonment and not being worthy of love, we will continue to be plagued by loneliness even when we find a new lover or friend.

If loneliness is an ongoing nagging emotion in your life, you can try to avoid it and dull it and sidestep it and overwhelm it, or you can deal with it directly, call its bluff and break out of its grip once and for all. Of course, you will sometimes encounter life situations that make you feel lonely for a short time, but you won't live continually under the pall of loneliness and fear of getting stuck all by yourself.

From our earlier conversations and programs, you already know what to do to face loneliness head-on.

1. Regularly take time to be alone with yourself, and just honestly observe what thoughts are dominating your mind when you feel lonely. Accept these thoughts and the feelings they're provoking.

2. Identify the one-liners that lie at the center of your feelings of loneliness, and use the de-beliefing technique taught earlier to shine the light of adult reason on your old assumptions and attitudes toward yourself and the world.

3. Establish new beliefs and assumptions about yourself and the world that reflect your adult abilities and reality. Regularly meditate upon these new attitudes, and notice when your mind begins to backslide into the old ones.

4. Steadily over the next weeks and months, develop a more loving, nurturing relationship with your own self. Question negative self-images you have been carrying, and create a new self-image in your mind that is centered in love, acceptance, and present-moment reality.

5. Choose to hold your focus of attention less in the past, less in chronic thought, and more in the unique unfolding of the present moment, where you can encounter new friends to fulfill your needs.

6. Regularly tune into your own heart, and choose to live your life focused upon your feelings in your heart. Allow your love for yourself to flow out into love for other people, so that wherever you are, you feel a member of the universal family of loving hearts throughout the world.

7. Whenever any "bad" emotion grips you, be it fear, anger, depression, loneliness or whatever, have the courage to face the emotion, accept it in the present moment, shine the light

of love and reason on it, quiet the negative thoughts that are stimulating the emotion, and bring yourself into the healing grace of the heartfelt present moment.

When you need direct techniques for overcoming thoughts and emotions that are making you suffer, please return to the specific sessions in earlier chapters or go to my website for additional specific support. For now, here's an enjoyable "peace when alone" meditation that you can do whenever you're alone and want to open up to your own present feelings, and attain a sense of peace and joy when alone.

GUIDED SESSION 5:
PEACE WHEN ALONE
•

Set aside ten minutes or so . . . get comfortable however you want to . . . and turn your attention toward your own present awareness. What's going on inside you? . . . Where's your attention? . . . Allow your thoughts and feelings and perceptions to happen, as you observe them coming and going through your mind . . .

Allow your jaw to relax . . . your tongue to relax . . . inhale through the mouth and yawn if you want to . . . stretch with your whole body . . . and let yourself relax completely . . . tune into the air flowing in and out your nose or mouth . . . the movements in your chest and belly as you breathe . . . and your heart, beating right in the middle of your breathing . . .

Without any judgment, begin to open up and feel whatever feelings are in your heart right now . . . breathe into them . . .

accept them . . . love them . . . let them soften . . . and begin to calm down . . .

Right now you have nowhere to go . . . nothing to do . . . you can relax and just hang out with yourself . . . notice how you feel inside, when you say to yourself, "Things are okay, just as they are right now." Stay aware of your breathing . . . let it soften and relax . . . make no effort to breathe . . . accept the world just as it is . . . everything's okay right now . . . you can ease up . . . open your heart . . . enjoy life . . .

And notice what feelings arise, when you say to yourself, "I'm okay, just as I am right now."

Stay aware of your breathing . . . your heart . . . your feelings throughout your body . . . and let yourself feel the good rush of opening your heart . . . to yourself . . . nowhere to go . . . nothing to do . . . opening to good feelings . . . just being . . . enjoying . . .

And when you're ready, you can let go of this guidance and stay tuned into your inner feelings . . . and without any forethought . . . without any effort . . . let yourself spontaneously, in the spirit of free play, just explore whatever experience comes to you now . . .

For streamed-audio guidance through this experience, go to www.johnselby.com.

chapter 6

insight at work

As you'll remember from reading thus far in this book, we started Chapter I with two quite different accounts of a businessman waking up in the morning and heading off to an important business presentation. In Richard's first account he was acutely worried about the future, emotionally tense and mentally buzzing, closed to heart-to-heart interaction with his wife and son, aggressive toward a fellow worker, and in general not very successful with his business presentation or his family life. He ended up feeling depressed, defeated, angry, worried, and hopeless.

We then explored how that disastrous morning of his could have flowed if he had learned the mind-management skills we're exploring in this book and these training programs. We saw him wake up and take time to make contact with his own feelings and heart center; we saw him quiet his busy thoughts so that he began the day feeling good in his body and joyous in his relationship with his wife and son. He then tapped into several deep business insights seemingly out of the blue – because he maintaining an expansive, intuitive state of mind. And at work, he did beautifully with his presentation and general communications, speaking from the heart and touching his colleagues deeply with his presence and ideas.

We then spent four chapters exploring the various elements that you can use to your advantage, in managing your mind so that your own life story flows harmoniously, successfully, and joyfully. We first learned the basic quiet-mind meditation to immediately silence the flow of thoughts through your mind. Then we delved deeply into the three primary inhibitors of a quiet, peaceful, insightful mind – judgment, anxiety, and a closed heart. You now know the most powerful self-help techniques for quieting judgmental thoughts, letting go of anxious thoughts, and opening your heart to the inflow of love and truth in your life.

Thus far we've seen how to apply these techniques to your solitary life, to improve your relationship with your self and transform lonely times into creative, enjoyable times alone. In this chapter and the next, we're going to show how the quiet-mind principles and techniques you're learning will serve you beautifully as you leave your solitary realms and venture into family, social, business, and intimate relating. Most of all, we're going to delineate how a quiet mind and open heart generate not only compassion and harmony, but also personal power and interpersonal dynamism.

Vital Preparations

As you have no doubt guessed by now, the first step in successfully moving out into the world to claim your fair portion of the universal wealth is to make sure that before you have your first encounter of the day, you have consciously assumed control of your own mind, and made the necessary shifts of consciousness to ensure that you're in optimum inner condition for a successful encounter.

I highly recommend that you begin to discipline yourself just enough to where each and every morning you set aside five minutes before heading out into the world, to clarify in your mind the priorities that you're going to hold to throughout the day. A five-minute meditation ritual each morning can transform your life – because you take the crucial inner step of choosing to focus your mind's attention beyond the usual flood of thoughts that assail you each morning, toward your present-moment consciousness of your deeper being.

When you discipline your mind for just five minutes each morning so that it focuses its full attention on the present moment, you activate an entire array of life possibilities that simply won't exist for you during the day if you remain unconscious of your deeper presence and power.

The guided session at the end of this chapter is especially designed to be experienced before you go to work so that you are in optimum mental position for success and enjoyment during the work day. The session helps you come fully into the present moment, with your thoughts quiet, then helps you open your heart to yourself and the people you'll interact with during the day, then allows you time to tap whatever intuitive insights might be wanting to rise to the surface related to your coming day. By taking five minutes each morning to move through this process, you'll enhance every aspect of your social, family, and business life.

Business with Heart

From your very first movement into the day, the primary challenge will be to see if you can lead with your heart in all your interactions, focusing on the spirit of cooperation rather than competition. Competition is very much a function of the primitive reptilian brain, where we see a danger to our personal survival and fight against that danger to defeat our opponent. Competition, by definition, is heartless and ruthless, devoid of any compassion for the opponent – and ultimately driven by fear.

Surely, we can play business in this heartless manner – but it's not going to fulfill us at deeper levels at all. Rather, we can enter into all business with our focus on cooperation, where we work together with other human beings for the good of all, in a spirit of compassion and shared enterprise. The key point here is that rather than letting fear drive us, we open up and allow love to impel our lives. Which is the greater life-supporting power, after all?

The proof is in the pudding. With every single person you encounter in the next twenty-four hours, for instance, notice if you are more successful with that person if you are afraid and therefore aggressive, judgmental, and defensive toward the person – or if you let go of your fears, open up, and relate in love and acceptance?

The answer is always the same – love wins out over fear every time, for all the reasons we've explored already. The executive who walks into a meeting radiating compassion, harmony, and a readiness to cooperate with the other people in the room is going to succeed far beyond the executive who walks into the room hostile, defensive, ready to do battle to defeat everyone he perceives as his enemy.

So when I suggest that you lead with your heart, I'm not setting you up to be eaten alive by the wolves. I'm setting you up to eliminate the atmosphere of dog-eat-dog wherever you go, so that good feelings dominate the atmosphere at work, and harmony prevails.

There will be times when you can enter the workplace and effortlessly stay in heartfelt emotions throughout the day. However, especially in the beginning, you'll find that you are packing an entire assortment of habitual judgments and attitudes and assumptions about your fellow workers, and also about yourself as a worker, that instantly generate contraction, competition, and disharmony. When you find yourself feeling any negative emotion in your heart, it's time to catch the thought or memory or busied assumption that is generating the emotion — and process that underlying thought so that it is no longer determining your mental and emotional condition in that situation.

To this end, the simple yet powerful little meditation I just gave you can work wonders, and it is important to do it every morning to actively identify negative feelings you may hold toward fellow workers, and consciously open your heart in acceptance of these people. Similarly, when you're in action at work and find that you're feeling hostile toward someone, or afraid in their presence, or judgmental about them — all you have to do is take a deep breath, choose to shift from judgmental thoughts to heartfelt feelings, and say silently: "I'm sorry I was judging you. I accept you just as you are and open my heart to you."

This inner statement of the intent to let go of judgmental thoughts toward a colleague at work seems simplistic, but if you've been doing the programs in this book, the words you say silently to this person will resonate throughout your being, waking up your ability to quiet judgmental thoughts at will, and open your heart to accept the world around you.

Work in the Present Moment

Work is definitely a thought-intensive affair for most of us. This book isn't in any way encouraging you to stop thinking altogether, certainly not at work. We've seen that the problem-solving analytical function of the human mind is an amazing and positive phenomenon that supports our entire world economy. Labor is basically the activating thought and resulting physical action required to make sure each and every day that people receive the material goods and services that they need or want. And in order for any action to happen, we first must entertain the idea of that action, the concept of carrying through with that action, and the communication to initiate that action.

However, in our prevailing scientific and cultural worship of the deductive process of the mind, we've tended to overlook certain psychological dynamics in the workplace that flash a red light of warning when we become overly caught up in deductive reasoning at work. Specifically, as we've seen, deductive reasoning is a past-future function of the mind where we process previous information from our memory databanks, analyze the information, and project a conceptual model of how that information might play out in the future. This is the function of problem solving in action. We traditionally hold such problem-solving mental activity as primary at work. There's a problem to solve – let's apply deductive mentation to come up with a solution.

However, if you take a close constant look at your workplace over the next few days, you'll notice that most of the time, except for rote data-entry work and the like, the primary activity at work isn't problem solving in which constant thinking is primary. The dominant activity in most businesses involves learning more about a situation, communicating about a situation, and brainstorming intuitively to gain a broader understanding of a situation.

We saw earlier that learning in itself is not a past-future cognitive function of the mind. Learning only takes place when we let go of our constant thoughts about past experiences, and tune into the actual perceptual information coming to us only in the present moment. The company that succeeds best will naturally be the company that is regularly tuning in to what's happening in the present moment so as to gain maximum information before doing the cognitive process of transforming the perceptual data into a meaningful concept.

Therefore it makes solid business sense to train everyone on a business team, no matter what their role, to regularly pop out of "thinking about" mode and shift into "seeing the truth of the matter" mode.

Hold in mind that deductive thinking is always, by definition, a function of the mind being focused on a point (word by word in linear progression) rather than stepping back and seeing the larger picture at once. I strongly recommend that in every workplace, everyone be encouraged, even guided directly once every half-hour, to pause for a few minutes from their fixation upon their particular item of concern, to relax and take a few deep breaths, shift into whole-body heart-centered attention in the present moment, and take in the whole of the situation.

Business is a process whereby a group of individuals agree to put their attention together during a certain period of time, to accomplish a shared goal. When individuals come together to work as a team, two things need to happen: They all need to maintain the greater vision of the goal so that they indeed work toward the same accomplishment, and each person needs to do what he or she does best by fixating on a particular aspect of the project.

A principal difficulty with most businesses that fail is that, as time goes by, individual team players tend to get so caught up in their special fixation on a part of the goal that they progressively lose touch with the greater vision. Another main difficulty with companies that fail to accomplish their goal is the erosion of performance and team spirit caused by fear-based thoughts and resultant emotions that begin to dominate the atmosphere of the workplace. The programs you're learning in this book will assure that these two primary dangers don't infect your business.

As a consultant, I've been brought into offices where the emotional atmosphere is so thick with anxiety, hostility, judgment, and rejection that it was a miracle that any work got accomplished in that company at all. Over time, hundreds of relatively small negative encounters had gone unaddressed, and worried thoughts had spread like a cancer throughout the minds of the workers – to where hearts were shut, minds were a confusion of hostile and upset thoughts, bodies were tense and unhealthy, and love was pretty much nonexistent.

In most cases, the solution to such a negative work atmosphere doesn't have to be firing everybody or putting everybody into therapy. The solution can be a gentle regular five-minute break, during which everyone is simply guided into feeling better in their bodies, quieting their thoughts altogether for long enough for good present-moment feelings to begin to arise, and encouraging everyone to focus on the shared vision of the company to work together in harmony, to accomplish a shared goal. I've never come across an office situation where rapid improvement of morale, performance, and creative action didn't emerge from teaching employees the fine art of regularly shifting from being fixated upon a point and lost in thought, to letting go of thinkaholic habits and enjoying the present moment, the whole, and responding spontaneously with their whole being.

A business is only as good as its employees. Employees who are encouraged to regularly take such a break and feel good in their hearts toward each other, and be receptive to what's happening around them in the present moment, perform better. And the hidden plus that is actually most important is that shifting into more productive mind states also happens to brighten spirits and make everyone feel better – which in turn promotes production and success in the company.

Freedom of Mind at Work

Many employers coming across programs such as those outlined in this book often become so enthusiastic that they want to make all of their employees go through the exercises.

However, I feel I should state clearly here that even though such programs might be very helpful not only for business but for the individual employee, I do not feel an employer has a right to impose any individual mind-management or cognitive-therapy training, or indeed any hourly or daily group training program, on employees. It's perfectly okay to provide a regular five-minute breather that allows and even guides employees into a more present-moment, enjoyable state of mind and body. However, a firm line must be drawn at work between simple relaxation breaks and concerted mind-management training.

Personal growth is a personal matter, not a company matter, in my opinion. I encourage employers to educate employees at work regarding the existence and benefits of mind-management programs such as the one you're learning here. I also encourage employers to provide time and funding for employees to attend training seminars, and to obtain at-home materials for self-help training. In this regard, the programs in this book are learned best at home anyway. They are inward-looking, reflective processes rather than group activities. However, it's extremely important that employees have total freedom to decide whether they want to participate in such programs, and not be penalized in any way if they choose not to.

Therefore my assumption will be that perhaps you share the short at-work five-minute breather break with your colleagues at work, and perhaps talk at leisure about the concepts introduced in this book as they apply to mental performance and problem solving on the job. But I assume that your actual studying and training to master these mind-management programs will be done by you at home, independent of company supervision.

Along with the regular training and reflection and healing you're doing on your own with the programs in this book, I'd like to present you with a special checklist you can run down each morning before heading to work and each evening after work (or whatever your daily schedule might be). Based on what you discover from this checklist, you will know where to focus special attention while at work, and also what particular programs you should focus on at home, to resolve the business worry, conflict, or dilemma you've found.

This is a simple format for evaluating various aspects of your work situation, in light of your own mind-management progress.

PRE-WORK CHECKLIST

1. Do you feel any apprehensions or worries related to work? If so, please write them down. Are you ready to resolve and let go of these worries?

2. Is there anyone at work that you don't like, or judge negatively? If so, state who the person is, and what the judgment is, and if it's really true. Are you ready to let go of these judgmental thoughts?

3. Are you out of harmony, in conflict with, angry at anyone at work? If so, state who the person is, and why. Are you ready to let go of your negative feelings, and open your heart in love and acceptance to this person?

4. Does your heart feel heavy, when you think of going to work? If so, state the underlying thoughts and assumptions making your heart feel heavy about work. Are you ready to let go of these negative thoughts?

5. Is your mind fixated upon trying to solve some problem at work? If so, state the problem. Are you ready to receive insight into this problem?

6. Is there something you'd like to change at work? If so, state what, and how. Are you ready to act to accomplish this change?

7. Do you feel good about your own presence at work? If not, state why. Are you ready to accept yourself at work, just as you are?

Quiet Mind at Work

Here's a general reference list for how to best participate in your at-work situation.

HEART FIRST: No matter whatever else you might be doing, remain aware of your heart. Whatever emotions come, accept them – and stay centered in your heart. This is your lifeline with your higher self, your spiritual presence, your loving power.

PRESENT MOMENT: No matter whatever else is happening, maintain at least some of your awareness focused on the present moment – by remaining conscious of your breathing, your heart, your wholebody in this present moment.

QUIET MIND: As often as possible, shift into full perceptual presence where you're aware of two or more sensory inputs at once – thus quieting your habitual thought-flows and bringing yourself powerfully into the present moment where your presence is felt directly by those around you . . .

FEAR NOT: Whenever you find yourself feeling anxious or defensive, realize that you're slipping into fear mode – and choose to let go of the future-based fear as best you can, by quieting the anxious thought, and tuning into present-moment feelings of compassion in your heart.

JUDGE NOT: As much as possible, quiet judgmental thoughts in your mind at work – so that you can accept the present moment just as it is, and thus empower yourself to participate in that present moment and help it evolve in positive directions . . .

PERCEIVE THE WHOLE: As often as possible, shift out of linear deductive mentation so that you can perceive the present moment as a whole, and respond with your whole being in the most appropriate spontaneous manner.

LET LOVE (AND MONEY) FLOW: By remaining focused on the present-moment evolution of the situation happening at your workplace, allow yourself to participate in the natural flow of the moment with love in your heart – so that you optimize both your own enjoyment of the moment, and the advancement of your company's goals.

Conscious at Work

The more conscious you are at work, the higher your success. The more conscious you are, the more loving you are. The more conscious you manage to stay, the more creative you will be. Here are questions you can regularly ask yourself at work, to evaluate if you're remaining in the light of present-moment awareness.

- Am I aware of my breathing?
- Am I centered in my heart?
- Is my mind clear?
- Am I feeling creative?
- Am I accepting?
- Am I participating?
- Am I here in my body?
- Am I feeling love?

GUIDED SESSION 6:
AT-WORK FIVE-MINUTE BREATHER

•

This short program is designed for one or more people at work, as a general relaxation/enjoyment/peace/insight opportunity to be used every half hour, every hour, or just once or twice a day as you prefer.

To quickly ease up, relax, and enjoy a few good deep breaths at work, just make sure you're comfortable . . . momentarily let go of whatever you've been working on . . . and shift your focus from thinking and doing, to feeling, and just being . . .

Let your eyes close if they want to, and if it feels good, turn your mind's attention to your breathing . . . make no effort to breathe . . . just feel the air flowing in your nose or mouth . . . and out your nose or mouth . . . let your shoulders relax . . . your jaw . . . your tongue . . . and give yourself permission to feel good in your body right now . . .

Go ahead and stretch if you want to . . . yawn . . . make any movements that feel good . . . sigh and make any sounds you want . . .

And now just relax completely . . . let your face muscles relax . . . notice the movements in your chest and belly as you breathe . . . and tune into how you feel right now, in your heart. If there's anyone you've been feeling upset with, you can let that tension go . . . and tune into a feeling of harmony in your workplace . . . where you're all working together today, for the common good . . .

And if you want to, you can now let your attention move effortlessly to your present project . . . and allow any insights to come to mind, as you see your project as a whole, in its entirety, and allow insights to flow . . .

For streamed-audio guidance through this experience, go to www.johnselby.com.

chapter 7

bliss in sexual passion

We saw earlier in this book that love is not experienced as a thought in our heads; love is a feeling in our hearts, and indeed throughout our bodies. In Chapter 4 we explored in depth how the human heart is not only a biological pump but also a most remarkable fifth brain with the unique capacity to transform our brain's perceptions and responses into organic feelings that impact us powerfully at physical and emotional and indeed spiritual levels of being.

In this chapter I'd like to share with you perhaps the deepest application of these quiet-mind techniques you're beginning to master. You'll remember how Nicole in Chapter 3 was able to transform her dating experience by quieting her worries, letting go of future projections, and centering her awareness in her heart as she approached a potential new lover and long-term mate. Several weeks later, she told me the following, which I've compressed here for brevity's sake.

That first evening together with Michael, we hardly touched. I was practicing what you'd taught me, about not pushing myself to do anything just because I might think I was supposed to – and so I didn't. I stayed fairly passive during dinner and afterward when we sat on his balcony and talked. He didn't seem in a hurry either; in fact I rather enjoyed a man who wasn't pushing me, who seemed to be staying in touch with his heart more than things down below.

We didn't even kiss good night when I left his house. I could feel all sorts of growing passion inside me, but I would have been leading with my ideas of what I should do, rather than my heart's feelings, if I'd made the move to kiss him that night. It all felt just so perfect, but so, well – bashful I guess, and nicely so.

I had to go out of town on business for three days, and when I got back we went to a play together that same night. The whole time I'd been gone, I'd felt growing feelings inside me, a hunger for him. And when he came to my door and picked me up, without even thinking about it, our bodies just came together into a long hug that felt so good, especially because it caught both of us by surprise, as if our bodies already knew what to do.

Well, that night was beautiful. We went to his place after dinner and the play and talked and talked, holding hands – but again there was that strange calmness inside me where I used to always be full of anxious thoughts about whether I was doing what I should be, to please him. Obviously I was strongly attracted to him and him to me, but this time I just refused to worry about whether I'd do something wrong and lose him. I'd learned how to quiet the usual thoughts that used to plague me, and instead I was just "there" with Michael.

Several times we just sat side by side and didn't say anything for minutes on end, listening to the birds, watching the moon come out from behind the clouds.

And believe it or not, even though I was almost swooning with passion for him, I left that night after just a few kisses. Something inside me wasn't ready to open up to him all the way, and I respected that feeling because it was a feeling in my heart, not some idea in my head. My mind was in fact warning me that if I wasn't more open to him sexually, I might lose him – but I just dunked that thought, and stayed centered where I found peaceful feelings.

The very next night he came over to my place with some Chinese food and a bottle of wine, and we ate hungrily on the living room floor, both of us feeling half-starved and gobbling with great pleasure, laughing at ourselves. And then I put on a CD of some classical music that I'd always loved, and we just lay there on our backs side by side and listened to the whole CD without saying anything, without moving. I felt as if I was in bliss, with nothing to do, absolutely nothing expected of me. The CD clicked off and time went by as if there were no time at all, just this unique feeling of having no pressures, no expectations, no sense of the future at all.

Right in the middle of that perfect stillness and quiet, without a single thought in my head, I rolled over on top of him and lay there, my head on his chest, listening to his heart. His hands came around me, and a passion I'd never known before came rushing through my body, a passion not driven by my usual ideas of how I should make love and what I should do next and what he might be thinking and how I should try to please him and how I wanted him to please me. There was just no thinking at all . . . and it happened so beautifully that we were both crying and laughing after we came . . . and afterward we lay there in each other's arms on the rug, again just being together, not doing anything, just floating in some new space where we were . . . together.

Where Passion Comes From

There was once a truly great doctor, scientist, and therapist named Wilhelm Reich who began his career in prewar Vienna. Because of his sexual honesty and experimentation into the nature of the human orgasmic response in his medical and psychiatric practice, along with his growing disregard for his early mentor Sigmund Freud, he found himself forced out of Vienna in the early 1930s. He moved to Berlin, where he continued experimenting with new therapy techniques grounded in his professional and personal search for a more spontaneous way through which to heal emotional wounds, break beyond the confines of programmed attitudes and beliefs, and learn to express passions and needs directly. However, he found himself unable to keep his mouth shut about his psychiatric opinion of Hitler, and had to flee to Scandinavia, where he again continued with his research into the nature of the human sexual response.

Soon Reich again had to relocate due to governmental pressure and censure of his life's work. He moved to the United States of America, where a growing group of psychiatrists and therapists supported his studies and ideas about sexuality and emotional healing. But during the early 1950s, conservative (perhaps more properly called reactionary) government and medical groups found his seemingly libertine sexual concepts and therapy practices dangerous, and on charges that were later found to be entirely trumped up, he was actually thrown into prison in 1953. A year later he died in prison, supposedly of a heart attack.

I was lucky enough to study with two of Wilhelm Reich's main students, Alexander Lowen, who started the highly successful bioenergetics therapy approach, and Charles Kelley, who founded the Radix Institute. Chuck especially impressed me with his techniques for liberating the human spirit from its programmed fears and cultural constrictions. I would like to dedicate this chapter to him and his work, because the insights herein originated with him, and of course with his own teacher, Wilhelm Reich.

The essence of Reich's and Chuck's therapy technique was to have clients lie down on their back on the floor and just do nothing – except breathe deeply through the mouth. What Reich had discovered was that the human organism, when given half a chance, would naturally begin to heal itself through the spontaneous release of emotions and the flood of memories and thoughts, beliefs and movements that accompanied the release of the pent-up emotions.

An entire generation of therapists from the 1950s to the 1970s was strongly influenced by Wilhelm Reich's basic realization that the human organism naturally shifts into a healing process when allowed to. This book, and the techniques described herein, is based on this understanding. And nowhere is it more important than in sexual relating. Indeed, for Reich and Kelley, the primary emotional and attitudinal healing mechanism of the human organism is the process we usually term the orgasm, where passion takes us over, we lose all sense of past and future, all thoughts stop, and we enter into a realm of consciousness where our emotions are released and healed, where we experience ourselves at least momentarily beyond the confines of our own beliefs, and our heart opens up to overwhelm our whole being with the power and glory of love.

A number of Reich's books are still in print, and if your own sexuality is of interest to you, I encourage you to read such primary books as *The Function of the Orgasm, The Bio-electrical Investigation of Sexuality and Anxiety,* and *Wilhelm Reich: Selected Writings,* as well as biographies of his controversial life, such as *Fury on Earth* by Myron Sharaf and the forthcoming book entitled *Wilhelm Reich: Psychotherapist and Radical Naturalist* by Robert Corrington. He was one of those geniuses who ended up half-crazy because of persecution and perhaps also because he pushed too far beyond the usual limits of human consciousness. Some of his more radical visions may prove too much to absorb – and I disagree with some of them myself – but his basic message about spontaneity and sexuality continues to ring true and inspire new generations.

The heart of that message was that we need not be driven by our logical minds in order to live a full life. Indeed, Reich insisted that we cannot live a full life until we learn to regularly shift out of the thinking manipulating mind, into functions of the mind where the whole being is choosing what to do, each and every new moment of the day.

Passion for Reich was what happens when we surrender mental control of our organism, and trust in our deeper self to choose the appropriate action. In the ultimate expression of passion, the orgasm, we find ourselves totally out of control, yet perfectly trustworthy, in bliss, and in harmony with the person we're making love with. When thoughts stop, the body still knows what to do – and does it with perfection and pleasure unknown to the thinking mind.

Sexual passion does not emerge from the activity of the

thinking mind. In fact, as soon as we start thinking, passion begins to retreat from the scene. Passion is a feeling in the heart and the genitals; it is a function of perceptions and feelings that probably predate our thinking minds by many thousands of years. More specifically, sexual passion happens as an integrated phenomenon when our full range of senses perceive a situation where we are free to let go of all fears and problems, as we shift into pure sensation and emotion.

To accomplish the full flush that leads to orgasm, the limbic and perceptual regions of the mind interact with the heart-mind and its vast potential, thus eliciting the flood of feelings of surrender, desire, and love throughout the body. We let go of who our self-image says we are, and surrender to who we really are.

Most of us hunger for this primal release on a regular basis, because it makes us feel so good as it quiets our usual worries and concerns, blows off pent-up emotions, opens our hearts – and at least momentarily shifts us into states of consciousness where we feel one with our sexual partner and with the entire universe.

PAUSE AND EXPERIENCE

•

Almost surely, you know the passion I'm talking about, where momentarily you're just "lost" to the everyday rational realms of consciousness, and thriving in the explosion of pleasure and knowingness, the oneness and wisdom of sexual intercourse. After reading this paragraph, close your eyes, tune into your breathing . . . your heart . . . your whole body . . . and allow memories to come to you of times when you were making love . . . and passion overwhelmed you . . .

When the Heart Rules

Unfortunately, all too often, even when we have the chance to make love with someone, we don't manage to quite surrender our ego presence enough to where the sexual magic happens. We might act out the physical movements of making love, but in the end all we did was have sex – the genitals did their release but the heart was not touched. We approached the ultimate, but didn't experience it.

If you're presently in a sexual relationship or moving into one, everything you've been learning in this book can be applied with great success to your lovemaking experience. And if you're not in a fulfilling sexual relationship but yearn for one, the programs in this book will serve as deep preparation as you make yourself ready for sexual union. My text *Sex and Spirit*, plus specific online programs, offer further guidance in this regard beyond the scope of this present book.

One thing is sure. Your childhood upbringing strongly conditioned you with beliefs about your sexuality and how you should behave sexually. However, most of such childhood programming related to sex ends up hindering true sexual union, rather than augmenting it. Let me state what seem to be the essential axioms to a truly fulfilling sexual life.

SEXUAL AXIOM 1: The key to deep sexual release lies in quieting the flow of thoughts through your mind while you're making love. Only when you let go of the past and the future, and surrender to the spontaneous unfolding of the present moment, can you truly experience the power and glory of sexual intercourse.

SEXUAL AXIOM 2: The real fulfillment in sexual intercourse comes only when the genital region of the body and the heart region of the body are integrated as one unified experience. The heart has its own orgasm, and this orgasm is essential for complete release, healing, and transcendence.

SEXUAL AXIOM 3: Contrary to popular cultural belief, indulging in sexual fantasies while making love doesn't aid in orgasm, but gets directly in its way – because fantasizing takes you away from the present moment and withdraws attention from your sensory interaction with your lover. Quieting the fantasy function of the mind is therefore important, for attaining true sexual union.

SEXUAL AXIOM 4: You cannot have a deep sexual experience when you're anxious or worried. Fear keeps you alert to the world around you and therefore unable to surrender to the inner realms of intercourse. You need to let go of your worries if you want to experience deep lovemaking.

SEXUAL AXIOM 5: You must put aside all judgment in order to attain orgasm. You must accept yourself just as you are, and your lover just as he or she is, if you want to merge in pure ecstatic joy and orgasm. Making love is just that – you're creating love through total acceptance and surrender to the inflow of the creative force through your merged bodies and hearts and souls.

SEXUAL AXIOM 6: In order to attain deep union and sexual fulfillment, you must be willing to let your emotions flow freely and heal during the act of love. As long as you're afraid to let your sexual partner see your buried emotions, you won't be able to experience total surrender to passion. Orgasm and emotional healing are one and the same thing – you can't have one without the other.

SEXUAL AXIOM 7: If you want to have fulfilling sexual intercourse, you cannot close your heart to experiencing your own
spiritual core of being. Making love means intimately experiencing the creator – you're plugging directly into the ultimate creative power of the universe when you make love.
From sexual intercourse, after all, comes the creation of a new
being. If you want to fully enter into the act of love, you must
have your heart open to your own infinite creative potential
and identity. Sex and spirit are, ultimately, one and the same.
At the moment of orgasm there is no boundary between you
and God or whatever name you use for the creator of this
universe and beyond. God is love . . . and orgasm is a primal
connection with our spiritual self.

What to Do in Bed

Nothing. Absolutely nothing.

When you're finally naked or mostly naked, lying beside
each other, do yourselves both a favor – don't do anything at
all. Just lie there, tune into your breathing, your heart, your
whole-body presence. Expand your awareness to include your
lover beside you; open your heart to feel his or her heart directly,
energetically. Let your thoughts become quiet, let your emotions calm down, and let go entirely of any notions in your
mind of what you should do next. Let the next movement of
your body happen spontaneously on its own.

And what if nothing happens at all? Perfectly okay. Just
stay with your breathing, and your inner sense of being connected with your own heart and its desires. Tune into whatever inner feelings are happening so that you become totally
consumed in your physical and emotional realms of being –
and see what happens.

Of course, there is a fear here, the fear that maybe you're

not really attracted to this person, or this person is not really sexually attracted to you. Therefore if you lie there and nothing happens, you'll have to confront this reality. This is a major fear – but it is best confronted immediately and directly, rather than forcing yourself to make love when the flow is not there. You'll save yourself a lot of heartbreak later on if you are honest from the beginning. When the flow's not there, do nothing. Don't push or you'll pay. Love is a flow, it's not a forced event. Let it come on its own. And always, accept reality – don't fight against the truth of the situation.

I know this will sound especially scary to those of you who are already in relationships. What if you lie there, and nothing happens, period? I've worked with quite a number of clients who have had this experience, and almost always, what happens when nothing happens is of great importance.

Very often, if nothing happens in bed, the two people will start talking. They'll share their feelings, their apprehensions. They'll confront each other honestly and begin to work out the beliefs, fears, attitudes, and fantasies that are standing between them coming together naturally.

Even if your partner isn't open at first to such self-reflection, you can do important detective work on your own later on. Take time alone, as you've learned already in Chapters 2 and 3, and ask yourself, "Why don't I want to make love with my lover?" Write down your reasons, which will usually be based on beliefs, attitudes, judgments, and fears – and then see if these beliefs and fears are real, and valid in your life.

In this process you'll discover a great deal about what holds you back in general from making love with passion and abandon, so that the next time you're in bed with your lover, you'll feel quite differently – and who knows what will happen? At least, you'll have grown, you'll be new.

Yes, it is true that sometimes couples discover through this technique that they are not attracted to each other, that they have been acting out a sham in bed with each other. But even this seemingly negative discovery is positive compared with continuing to live a lie with each other, feeling empty and more alone than ever after having sex without making love. When honesty rises up, it brings with it the great opportunity for change and growth. Who knows what the outcome of seeking and accepting the truth will be – but we absolutely must live our lives with integrity and honesty, especially at the intimate level, or life ends up hardly worth living at all.

In an honest evaluation of love in our society, most people get into bed with their partner and immediately start doing the things they think the other person wants done, the things that will stimulate sexual response. Their minds are the opposite of quiet – they're buzzing with thoughts of what they should do, with judgments of themselves and their partner's performance, with worries about the future or concerns of the past.

I realize that it's a major challenge to quiet your mind when you're in bed with your lover. You probably have a long personal history of anxiety related to sexual intercourse. All the various difficulties in quieting the mind that we've discussed in this book rise up strongly during romantic interaction. We're vulnerable, we're exposed, we're on the line, we're uncertain, we're confused, we're upset, we're just driven crazy with apprehensions that range from the embarrassingly simple to the frighteningly sublime.

What to do?

Here's one option now available to you – either by reading the following flow of suggestions and then applying them in bed, or listening together to the flow of suggestions, you can rapidly learn to let nature move you sexually in bed. If your lover agrees, you can do the following together.

GUIDED SESSION 7:

SEXUAL MEDITATION IN BED

•

You're relaxing together . . . for a few moments, not doing anything at all . . . just tuning into your own breathing . . . the air flowing in and out . . . without any effort . . . your heart beating in the middle of your breathing . . .

Without doing anything, you can become enjoyably aware of your skin . . . your whole body, lying on the bed . . . let your thoughts fade away . . . become entirely calm and quiet . . . make no effort to breathe . . . make no effort to do anything . . . just enjoy doing nothing . . . be at peace with yourself . . . and with your partner . . . nowhere to go, nothing to do . . .

And in this calm, accepting, peaceful state, allow your awareness to expand gently at its own pace, to begin to include the presence of your lover lying beside you . . . open your heart, to feel your lover's heart . . . its feelings, its passions, beating beside you . . . let your sexual desire begin to glow right at the center of your being . . . in your heart . . . in your breathing . . . in your muscles, in your genitals . . . allow nature to move you . . . accept whatever comes . . .

Breathe into a total surrender to your sexual desire . . . and begin to tune into the desire of your sexual partner beside you . . . allow the natural attraction of your two bodies, of your two souls, to move you . . . when the time is right, if the time is right, toward each other . . .

No need to think about what to do with each other . . . no need to do anything . . . just allow the perfection of the present moment to fill you, and perhaps spontaneously move you . . . and fulfill you both . . .

For streamed-audio guidance through this experience, go to www.johnselby.com.

chapter 8

a good night's sleep

On any given night, somewhere between 30 and 50 percent of our population will have difficulty falling and staying asleep. In a recent survey of 1,000 households in Los Angeles, a third of those polled indicated that they had current problems falling and staying asleep at night. A Gallup poll found a full 50 percent of the people interviewed "had trouble falling asleep or staying asleep." A study conducted in Florida by psychiatrist Ismet Karacan that surveyed 1,645 people, found that one-third of the population suffered from bouts of sleeplessness. Furthermore, as Philip Goldberg and Daniel Kaufman note in their excellent book *Everybody's Guide to Natural Sleep:* "It is also estimated that half of those not considered insomniacs have a sleepless night on occasion, and a large but undetermined number do not sleep as efficiently as they should."

In other words, getting a good night's sleep is a universal challenge that the majority of us struggle with on a nightly basis, often unsuccessfully. Doctors and psychologists have identified a variety of possible reasons for sleeplessness, and a great many good books have been written on self-help treatment for the condition. After studying the treatment of sleeplessness with Dr. Frances Cheek early in my professional work, and exploring improved treatment methods in my practice, I've also recently logged in with my *Secrets of a Good Night's Sleep* book and CD and a number of online audio-guidance sleep programs. Sleep fascinates me. We spend nearly a third of our lives sleeping, and we suffer greatly when regular sleep eludes us. Therefore a solid understanding of our nocturnal realms of consciousness is both fascinating and essential to a good life.

From reading this far into the present book, and beginning to learn to observe and quiet your thoughts at will, you're actually in a perfect position to cut through all the more superficial discussions and treatments of insomnia, and look directly to the root cause of disturbed sleep. Put simply, from my understanding, sleeplessness is usually caused by all the various upsetting thoughts running through our minds as we get into bed – thoughts that, as we've seen, in turn generate all the various emotional and physical symptoms that upset our lives, and disturb our sleep.

You already have in hand the mental tools for quieting such habitual thought-flows. If sleeplessness is an issue in your life, you'll want to devotedly master the programs that help you observe your chronic thoughts, especially just before you go to bed and while lying in bed – and then apply whichever particular programs seem best for putting your anxious thoughts to rest.

For some of you, just lying on your back and moving through the quiet-mind meditation you learned in Chapter

1 will be sufficient to let you calm your mind and slip into sleep. At bedtime you'll find it effective to listen to the audio-guidance session at the end of this chapter for extra support. Once you begin watching your mental habits just before you go to sleep, you'll also start to spontaneously self-correct the noisy patterns that stir up your emotions right before bed. To see the cause of the problem is often to transcend the problem.

However, for quite a number of you, your mental habits and resultant patterns of worrying just before bed will be so ingrained that you'll need to apply some stronger techniques to overcoming insomnia. I'll review these programs, which you've already learned, and as needed, you can go back and continue training your attention over the next few days and weeks to fully master the process. The good news is that all the mental explorations and practice you've already done in this book for quieting your mind directly apply to quieting your mind just before sleeping – so you're more than halfway there already.

For most of you, a bit of mental detective work, along with some de-beliefing, emotional healing, and heart opening, should provide you with the help you need to improve your sleep experience considerably. Do take full advantage of the various free online sleep programs as well, available at www.johnselby.com.

For those of you who find that this isn't enough help, please consider one-on-one counseling. Sleep disorders, when untreated over time, can seriously disrupt your entire life. You can go online and read about the various types of professional help available in your area, and choose which seems best for you.

A bit of advice I would like to offer those of you with serious insomnia problems: Sleeping pills are not the answer. Although traditionally otherwise helpless to do something about the condition, most doctors agree. According to Dr. Ernest Hartman, director of the Sleep Disorders Center at Tufts University School of Medicine, "Most sleeping pills are dangerous substances and have been overused . . . insomnia is not an illness for which a sleeping pill is a cure. Most often the cause will be behavioral or psychiatric (anxiety or depression) or medical."

In this light, logic clearly dictates reasonable pathways for resolving sleepless nights. If your condition is medical (a physiological problem causing bothersome pain or other sleep-disturbing conditions), do see your doctor for treatment. If your condition is psychological, let's apply the programs in this book to treat the underlying anxiety or depression. And if the book and audio programs aren't sufficient to overcome the problem, seek cognitive therapy.

Primary Causes of Insomnia

There is no longer any mystery concerning the main causes of sleeplessness. Let me list them here, together with the most effective treatment, and you can evaluate your own situation and act accordingly:

WORRIES: Going to bed with your mind full of worried thoughts is definitely the primary cause of insomnia. Perhaps you're worried about losing your job, about your health, about a relationship, about terrorists, about paying the rent – whatever you're worried about, you need to deal with the worries rather than take them to bed with you. When you're anxious, your nervous system is on alert because you're feeling threatened. And when you're in danger, it's not a good idea to doze off. You must deal with your worries and quiet them if you want to sleep well. We've said a lot about anxiety in this book. It all applies to the sleep experience too.

EXCITEMENT: Often we can't fall asleep because we're too excited about something happening the next day, or sometime in the future. Our minds are caught up in imaginings of the future, and these imaginings are stimulating our nervous systems and keeping us awake. The obvious cure for this is to focus not on the future but on the present moment. Perhaps put on a relaxation CD, stop thinking about what's coming, and focus on just being in the here and now . . . breathing . . . relaxing . . . aware of your toes . . . your hands . . . your whole body, here and now . . .

ENVIRONMENTAL STRESS: A dog barking in the distance, a neighbor playing unsoothing music, especially any unusual sounds at night, can throw your nervous system off kilter. The secret to dealing with environmental stressors is, first of all, to examine the assumptions that underlie your thinking ("I can't ever get to sleep when dogs are barking," for example). Let go of those beliefs – and then shift your focus of attention away from listening to two or more sensory inputs that aren't related to sound. For instance, focus on your breathing, your heart, your whole-body presence. Or while you stay aware of your breathing, also imagine something repetitive, such as the proverbial sheep jumping over a fence.

IRRITATION AND PAIN: Both temporary and chronic insomnia are sometimes caused by physical pain. Any health condition that has a physical dimension – a plugged-up nose, a sinus headache, skin allergies, a painful bruise or cut – can disturb your sleep. The only remedy for such temporary conditions tends to be the passage of time – and patience. But shifting your attention to your breathing and heartbeat can work wonders for many of these minor ailments, as well as letting go of thoughts such as, "I can never get to sleep when I have a cold." For long-term pain problems, dealing effectively with all the assumptions you have about your condition and getting to sleep will prove very helpful.

STRESS FROM WORK: A great many of us carry our business concerns home with us, by continuing to think about our at-work problems when we get ready to sleep. You can definitely put a halt to business problem solving when you go to bed. Just observe your thoughts, see that you have the habit of mulling over work problems in bed, and then quiet those thoughts by shifting into the present-moment experience of lying in bed, relaxing, breathing, and sleeping.

CAFFEINATED DRINKS: There is a direct link between certain items we eat and drink and a resulting inability to fall asleep. Any drink with caffeine in it, for instance, will keep you awake, no question. People who drink five cans of diet cola or chai tea or any other caffeine drink, and then find they can't fall asleep, will sleep much better if they change their choice of drinks.

EVERYDAY DRUGS: Likewise, many prescription medications such as mood elevators and diet pills will also keep you awake. Ask your doctor for further consultation on this. A great many over-the-counter medications are loaded with chemicals – caffeine, to name one – that won't let the nervous system relax and sink into a good sleep. And of course, drugs such as cocaine and amphetamines are known for the sleeplessness they cause.

Check your drug intake of all kinds, and take the rational steps to get a better night's sleep.

REJECTION AND ABANDONMENT: Many people can't fall asleep because they're feeling rejected or abandoned by a lover, a parent, a group, their workplace, or some other organization they felt bonded with. Such separation anxiety, or fear of abandonment, is a primal fear, as we have seen. Please work diligently with the programs in Chapter 3 if you are caught in bed tense with feelings of rejection and heartbreak. You'll need to reassure yourself that you can survive, you can take care of yourself, and you can love yourself and find new love, if you're ever going to sleep enjoyably again.

DEPRESSION: When we feel that we're no good and everything's hopeless in life, then getting to sleep is very difficult – because the underlying beliefs generating our depressed thoughts and feelings are telling us that we can't survive, we can't carry on – and this basic assumption will keep us awake for fear of actually ceasing to exist at all. Again, it's time for some serious homework related to your chronic thoughts at all times during the day. Depressive thoughts do have a way of rising to the fore when we are ready to go to bed and are done with the day. I recommend that, for one week or so, you write down the thoughts you think when you're in bed, really get to know the underlying thoughts that are polluting your mind and keeping you awake. Then apply the cognitive tools of this book and the free online guidance programs to transcending the beliefs that are making you suffer and not get to sleep. Probably you can cure yourself. If all else fails, do seek professional one-on-one help.

FEAR OF DEATH: The ultimate separation anxiety we face is of course our own demise, where our ego will probably dissolve as our deeper spiritual identity and consciousness move through the utter mystery of what comes after physical death. Many children experience temporary insomnia around the age of 11, for instance, when they first encounter the reality of death as a personal possibility. And we all get caught worrying about what's going to happen when we die, at least now and then. Again, the solution lies in observing exactly what thoughts we're thinking about death and the underlying assumptions we believe in concerning death. Also, please note that worrying about death is clearly a future-projection act of the mind. If you bring yourself into the perceptual-intuitive realms of consciousness in the present moment, you will quiet your worries and let go of the future fear.

PAUSE AND EXPERIENCE

•

Take a few moments after reading this paragraph to tune into your breathing . . . your heart . . . your whole-body presence . . . and then look back over the list of eight primary causes of insomnia and see which ring most true for you. Decide what action to take to begin to let go of sleepless nights and enjoy the bliss of deep sleep. And whenever you can't sleep, you can also put on the *Good Night's Sleep* CD and let the voice and music lead you into sleep.

Sleep-Well Checklist

Here's a short list I often hand out to clients and students that will help you make sure, just before going to bed, that you aren't heading to bed with a mind buzzing with tensions that will keep you up.

ARE YOU FEELING ANGRY AT ANYONE?

If not, great. If so, name the person, then take a deep breath or two, let your emotions calm down, your thoughts calm down, tune into your own heart, and say: "I accept what happened with that person, and I let go of that anger." Take a few more breaths, until you're breathing freely in the present moment, without carrying any negative thoughts to bed with you.

If this short process works, great. If not, return to Chapter 2 and the techniques outlined in "Negative Core Beliefs" for letting go of negative judgments against other people.

ARE YOU FEELING UNEASY, APPREHENSIVE, WORRIED, OR ANXIOUS?

If not, great. If so, say what you're worried or uneasy about, and then notice that between now and tomorrow morning, this danger almost certainly isn't going to bother you, so you can let go of the apprehension for tonight, and get a good night's sleep. Tune into the present moment where everything's okay. Let go of your thoughts about the future, and relax into some good feelings in your body. The sleep session at the end of this chapter will be of great help in this.

If this short process works, again – great. If not, please turn to Chapter 3, and for the next few days, make the techniques taught in that chapter most important to you, so that you can go to bed without worries plaguing you.

ARE YOU EXCITED ABOUT ANYTHING?

If not, great. If so, realize that this excitement will keep you awake as it floods your system with hormones that charge you for action. You will want to choose consciously to let go of the thoughts and future imaginings that are exciting you, and surrender to the relaxation that is found here in the present moment, in your whole body. Focus on your breathing, your heart, your toes, your hands, your whole body here in this present moment – and let the guided session lull you into a deep, satisfying sleep.

If this works, dandy. If not, you'll want to return to Chapter 1, and maybe Chapter 3, for additional help. Hold in mind that excitement always carries an edge of anxiety about what's going to happen to you in the future, so deal with that anxiety while also directly acting to quiet the flow of thoughts through your mind.

ARE YOU FEELING LONELY OR BROKEN-HEARTED?

If not, great. If so, notice that these feelings are activated by memories of the past and thoughts about the future. Choose to let go of your focus on past and future, for now at least. Accept the present moment just as it is, and tune into your love for your own self. Focus on your own bodily presence in the here and now as you open your heart to yourself, let your love flow out to the universe, and relax your heart into acceptance, love, and peace.

If this works for you, off you go to enjoyable sleep. If not, please find time in the next days to look deeply into Chapter 4, as you heal old heart wounds and move toward accepting and loving yourself just as you are, as your own best friend. Regularly notice when you think thoughts that make you feel lonely – and choose to quiet those thoughts in favor of present-moment activities that make you feel good. This freedom of choice is everyone's ultimate salvation in life.

IS ANYTHING IN YOUR SLEEPING ENVIRONMENT BOTHERING YOU?
If not great. If so, either deal with it – or accept it. And as you accept the bother, shift your focus of attention away from the sensory input, and toward enjoyable realms of experience. Especially tune into your own bodily feelings. Move your toes, perhaps move your pelvis a little, tense and then relax your whole body, and let yourself settle into inner realms of feeling that you enjoy, as you watch your breathing slowing down with each breath, until you drift off into a deep sleep.

HAVE YOU TAKEN ANY CAFFEINE PRODUCTS IN THE LAST FEW HOURS, OR ANY DRUGS OF ONE KIND OR ANOTHER THAT WILL KEEP YOU AWAKE?
If not, great. If so, tomorrow you may want to be more conscious of what you're choosing to take into your body that might keep you awake. If you find your mind and body revved up just before bed, you will benefit greatly from doing ten to fifteen minutes of exercises, walking, dancing, or any other physical activity that will blow off the energetic charge and let you then relax into sleep.

ARE YOU FEELING DEPRESSED?
If not, great. If so, patiently look directly to that feeling inside you, and as you watch it, see what thoughts emerge from the center of the feeling. Let those thoughts be there for a short time, and then say to yourself, "I don't want to have those thoughts anymore," and choose to shift your mind's attention elsewhere. Perhaps say to yourself, "Everything's okay," or "I let it all go." And then shift your focus of attention toward what's happening in the present moment – your own breathing especially. Make no effort to breathe. Let your

breathing stop and then start of its own volition, and let new life come flowing in as you relax, and surrender to sleep.

Hopefully, this process will be all you need, along with some audio guidance perhaps. For those of you who are chronically depressed, please return to the beginning of this book and master the programs for quieting depressive thoughts. And do seek outside help where needed.

ARE YOU FEELING GOOD AND CONTENT AND READY FOR SLEEP?
If so, great – down you go!

Movement Before Bed

A great many people head for bed packing muscular tensions in their bodies that need release. Hold in mind, as we've seen already, that upsetting thoughts (anger, anxieties, etc.) generate a flow of hormonal messages throughout the body to prepare the muscles to be ready for instant action to deal with whatever problem your mind is fixated upon. If you get into bed with your muscles still charged for action, sleep will elude you.

Consider doing just five minutes of movement before bed if sleeplessness is a regular problem for you. And always before getting into bed, stand a moment and just check out your bodily condition. If you're not feeling physically like sinking into deep relaxation and sleep, movement is the answer. As human beings we are clearly defined by our need for, and desire for, regular movement. We know we're alive by the movements of our breathing and hearts. We will know we're dead when we simply aren't moving anymore. To live is to move. Yet most of us don't move much during the day. If insomnia is a problem for you, I strongly recommend getting out and walking for half an hour to an hour a day, or doing some other enjoyable movement on a regular basis – it's one of the true sources of pleasure in life.

Before going to bed, you might want to put on some slow music that you love, and move to the music to release tensions in your body. Make sure that the music is relaxing and slow, and that you give yourself permission to enjoy yourself. Don't push yourself into movement, just stand a moment, listen to the music, and notice that you're already moving with your breath movements. Allow movement, however slight at first, to come on its own, and this will lead you into a deep relaxing flow of movement that will leave you ready to fall into bed satisfied with the movement of the day.

Don't force yourself to do particular motions – let the body be free to act spontaneously, at least once during the day before sleep. Our bodies are such amazing workhorses – they do what the mind orders them to do, constantly. Often our deductive minds push us to go in directions during the day that our deeper self really would prefer not to move in. This creates muscular and, indeed, spiritual tensions that need to be released before bedtime. Free spontaneous movement of any kind will bring your body, your spirit, and your mind into rapid harmony, and ready you for deep relaxation and sleep.

And of course, movement is present-moment stimulation that will naturally focus your mind's attention on the here and now, on two or more sensations at the same time. We've seen that this simple refocusing act automatically quiets the flow of thoughts through your mind. Whenever you want to silence bothersome thoughts, all you have to do is move – just get up and move!

PAUSE AND EXPERIENCE

•

Try this for yourself right now: After reading this paragraph, put the book down and sit for a moment, watch your breathing, tune into your whole body, and then choose to stand up. Move into an open area of the room or outside, and just stand a moment, tuning into your whole body in the present moment . . . and allow movements to come on their own. . . . See how good it feels to let your body move spontaneously!

Meditation

Many people find the best cure for insomnia is a regular evening meditation practice, where they sit quietly for half an hour or so, quiet their minds, still their emotions, and enter a state of inner peace and acceptance of life. I heartily encourage you to explore such a meditative cure for insomnia, in whatever particular meditative tradition you feel most attracted to. My website will also offer you several meditation techniques that you can master readily, through streamed-audio guidance.

You might have noticed that this book has barely mentioned the word "meditation" up till now. This is because the aim of the book has been to present a purely psychological approach to quieting your mind and opening your heart to the present moment. However, before ending this discussion, I do want to clarify that there are a great many meditation techniques and traditions in the world, yet all of them lead toward just one primal process and experience – that of quieting the mind, opening the heart, and tuning into the deeper universal truths and experiences of life. This book and its set of techniques, and the associated free online guided audio programs, fully accomplish this meditative goal, within the conceptual framework of psychological healing and growth.

Therefore, if you've begun to master the basic quiet-mind techniques of this book, you've begun to master meditation. By whatever name, you're learning to quiet your mind, look inward, open your heart, and receive deep wisdom and peace beyond your talkative ego mind.

Often a regular nighttime relaxation routine that you memorize and go through just before sleep, or a recorded guiding voice and relaxing music, can be of great help in breaking beyond old insomniac habits and mastering the fine art of falling effortlessly to sleep each new night. Here is the primary guided process that I've found covers all vital presleep steps. You'll find the free streamed-audio program at both the "Quiet Your Mind" and "Sleep Tonight" areas of www.johnselby.com.

GUIDED SESSION 8:

A GOOD NIGHT'S SLEEP

•

Once you've moved through the sleep-well checklist , and perhaps done some movements to discharge any remaining muscular tensions from the day, go ahead and relax in bed. You might want to start lying on your back if this is comfortable, and the let your body move into your various favorite positions later on . . .

Notice how your body feels right now . . . watch your breaths coming . . . and going . . . and coming again . . . without any effort at all . . . put your right hand on your belly, and your left hand over your chest . . . and experience the breathing movements under each hand, at the same time . . .

Tune into your heart under your left hand . . . accept whatever feelings you might find in your heart tonight . . . notice if your heart feels heavy or light . . . let go of any heaviness . . . let your thoughts go . . . let your emotions go . . . and say to yourself, "I open my heart to receive . . . acceptance . . . joy . . . love . . . peace . . . "

Just watch your breaths gently coming . . . and going . . . let your breaths stop when they want to . . . and start when they want to . . . zero effort . . . free . . . relaxed . . . feeling good . . .

Allow your awareness to include your heart . . . your hands . . . your feet . . . move your toes and feet a bit . . . now let them relax . . . move your fingers . . . and now let your hands relax . . . open your mouth and yawn if you want to . . . stretch . . . move your pelvis a little . . . relax . . . move your head gently back and forth a few times . . . relax your neck and shoulders . . . your tongue, your jaw . . . tense your whole body one last time . . . and now relax completely . . .

Your body is relaxed . . . your thoughts calm . . . emotions at rest . . . your breaths are coming . . . and going . . . slowly . . . peacefully . . . a warm inner feeling of peace . . . contentment . . . and soft relaxing love . . . flowing throughout your being . . .

You're just here . . . breathing . . . enjoying the music . . . letting go . . . surrendering to sleep . . . more and more . . . trusting . . . drifting . . . sleep . . .

For streamed-audio guidance through this
experience, go to www.johnselby.com.

Last Words

We've covered a great deal of ground in this book, compressing many different ideas, disciplines, and techniques into a single unified conceptual and practical approach to perhaps the most important issue of our lives – how we manage our own minds, moment to moment, to our best advantage. I thank you for following this flow of logic to the end, and thus gaining a sense of the whole.

Reading through this book is, of course, just the beginning. There will be one, two, or three chapters, maybe four or five, that speak most directly to you. And your next step in the days, weeks, and months that come will be to return to the chapters and programs that are most important to master and work with them until you make them truly your own. The goal is to integrate these mental procedures into your everyday consciousness so that wherever you are, whatever you're doing, you can readily quiet your mind and maintain the optimum consciousness for both thriving and enjoying every moment along the way.

I have been working with these particular mind-management techniques for many years now, and every day I regularly use them to keep my own mind focused where I prefer, and my own heart singing a bright song. Personal growth and awakening are lifelong enterprises. We're always learning, always opening, always discovering new depths of life to explore and embrace.

Blessings on your own life journey, and may these pages and audio programs support your growth for the duration! I look forward to getting to know you better online and during my seminar tours, and will continue to bring you all the new insights and techniques as they emerge.

Go for it!
John

Recommended Reading

There are other wonderful books you might want to read related to the theme of "quiet your mind." Listed below are some of the essential texts that helped clarify, reinforce, and inspire my own understanding of this deep theme – most of these books are at your library, and will make very worthwhile reading!

Austin, John, *Zen and the Brain,* MIT Press, Cambridge, MA, 1998.

Beck, Judith, *Cognitive Therapy,* Guilford Press, New York, 1995.

Bhante, Gunarantana, *Mindfulness in Plain English,* Wisdom Publishers, Boston, 1993.

Bohm, David, *Wholeness and the Implicate Order,* Routledge, Boston, 1980.

Castaneda, Carlos, *Journey to Ixlan: A Separate Reality,* Ballantine, New York, 1972.

Chalmers, David, *The Conscious Mind,* Oxford University Press, New York & London, 1996.

Childre, Doc, *The HeartMath Solution,* HarperSF, SanFrancisco, 1999.

Damasio, Antonio, *The Feeling of What Happens,* Harcourt Brace, New York, 1999.

Dozier, Rush, *Fear Itself,* St. Martins, New York, 1998.

Einstein, Albert, *Out of My Later Years,* Philosophical Library, New York, 1950.

Freud, Sigmund, *The Future of an Illusion,* W. W. Norton, New York, 1927.

Gendlin, Edward, *Focusing,* Bantam, New York, 1981.

Goldberg, Philip, *The Intuitive Edge,* Tarcher, Los Angeles, CA, 2003.

Hendricks, Gay, *Conscious Living,* HarperSF, San Francisco, 2000.

Huxley, Aldous, *The Perennial Philosophy,* Meridian, New York, 1970.

Jung, Carl, *Memories, Dreams, Reflection,* Fontana, New York, 1995.

Kornfield, Jack, *A Path with Heart,* Bantam, New York, 1993.

Krishnamurti, J., *The Limits of Thought,* Routledge, London, 1999.

Ledoux, Joseph, *The Emotional Brain,* Touchstone, New York, 1996.

Mckay, Matthew, *Thoughts and Feelings,* New Harbinger, Oakland, CA, 1996.

Miller, William, *Flash of Brilliance,* Perseus Books, Reading, MA, 1999.

Mitchel, Stephen, *The Enlightened Heart,* Harper & Row, New York, 1989.

Mitchell, Stephan, *The Enlightened Mind,* HarperCollins, New York, 1991.

Naranjo, Claudio, *The Psychology of Meditation,* Viking Press, New York, 1971.

Naranjo, Claudio, *The Psychology of Meditation,* Viking Press, New York, 1971.

Newberg, Andrew, *Why God Won't Go Away,* Ballantine, New York, 2001.

Nhat Hanh, Thich, *Breathe! You Are Alive,* Parallax Press, Berkeley, CA, 1996.

Nhat Hanh, Thich, *Present Moment, Wonderful Moment,* Parallax Press, Berkeley, CA, 1990.

Pert, Candace, *Molecules of Emotion,* Touchstone, New York, 1997.

Peurifoy, Reneau, *Anger,* Kodansha Press, New York, 1999.

Pinker, Simon, *How the Mind Works,* W. W. Norton, New York, 1997.

Radin, Dean, *The Conscious Universe,* HarperSF, San Francisco, 1997.

Rogers, Carl, *On Becoming a Person,* Houghton Mifflin, Boston, 1961.

Rosenberg, Larry, *Breath by Breath,* Shambhala, Boston, 1999.

Russell, Bertrand, *Mysticism and Logic,* Anchor Books, New York, 1957.

Russell, Peter, *Waking Up in Time,* HarperSF, SanFrancisco, 2003.

Shermer, Michael, *How We Believe,* Freeman, New York, 2000.

Snyder, Gary, *The Practice of the Wild,* Farrar, Straus & Giloux, New York, 1990.

Targ, Katra, *The Heart of the Mind,* New World Library, Novato, CA, 2000.

Teasdale, William, *The Mystic Heart,* New World Library, Novato, CA, 1999.

Tolle, Eckhardt, *The Power of Now,* New World Library, Novato, CA, 1998.

Watts, Alan, *The Spirit of Zen,* Murray, London, 1955.

Welwood, John, *Awakening the Heart,* Shambala, Boston, 1983.

Online Audio-Guidance Support

For each of the basic programs in this book, you can go to the author's community website at www.johnselby.com and gain free access to his professional presentation of the audio programs via streamed audio or download formats. Inexpensive CD versions of the audio programs are also available via online ordering. The primary *Quiet Your Mind* audio CD can also be purchased via mail by sending $16.00 (includes postage and handling) to: John Selby, Quiet Your Mind, P.O. Box 861, Kilauea, HI 96754.